praise for

HEART TOOLS FOR COUPLES

"This is an immensely accessible and practical book for couples. Full of illustrations and exercises, any couple who decides to practice these basic processes cannot but experience an amazing, compassionate relationship. I recommend it to all couples."

Harville Hendrix, Ph.D.
Author of *Getting the Love You Want: A Guide for Couples*

"If you're looking for the keys to greater depth and intimacy, this wonderful book offers simple but profound tools that will bring your relationship to a new level—and just might change your life. I've watched Ani and Bill apply these techniques to their clients and to their own lives for over two decades, and have seen how they walk their talk, with a thriving relationship to prove it. By practicing the tools in this book, you can have that too."

Anodea Judith, Ph.D.
Author of *Eastern Body, Western Mind* and *The Global Heart Awakens*

"The book is terrific. It offers a clear and practical roadmap to help you become the best partner you can be. The payoff is a relationship resilient enough to weather the hard times and romantic enough to open your heart and bring you joy every day."

Susan B. Lord, MD
Kripalu Center for Yoga and Health

"Bill and Ani Grosser have created a wonderful guide for actually living a more loving life. This easy to read, easy to use book not only talks about what it means to love, but actually helps couples to experience themselves and their partners as loving. By using vulnerable examples from their own many year marriage, Bill and Ani offer us a window into how to manifest the relationship of our dreams. Barbara and I have already integrated these practices and in the short month since we began, our level of openhearted connection has been enriched tremendously."

Maya Kollman, MA
Imago Therapy Master Trainer

HEART
TOOLS
for
COUPLES

HEART
TOOLS
for
COUPLES

8 ways to a loving relationship

BILL GROSSER *and* ANI NADLER GROSSER

Cover design by Gabrielle Senza
Book design by Emma Schlieder

Printed in the United States of America

The Troy Book Makers • Troy, New York • thetroybookmakers.com

To order additional copies of this title, contact your favorite
local bookstore or visit www.tbmbooks.com

ISBN: 978-1-61468-201-1

*We dedicate this book to
Allison and Greg, Derek and Jude,
and to our grandson, Julian.*

CONTENTS

◇◇◇◇◇◇◇◇◇◇◇◇◇◇◇◇◇◇◇◇◇◇◇◇◇◇◇◇◇◇

APPRECIATIONS

We wish to appreciate our family, friends, and clients, who have been our teachers and taught us lessons in many areas of life. We have laughed together, cried together, played together and, on occasion, struggled together.

We wish to thank Marian Sandmaier and Laura Didyk for editing our book. And thanks to our friends who read the book and gave us honest critique and encouragement: Darlene Graham, Steve Small, Kit Patten, Rosa Zubizarreta, Margie Hernandez, Oralee Stiles, and Linda Marshall. We want to thank Marsha Bernstein and Michael Madison for graciously offering us their mountain-top studio, with its magnificent vistas of the Hudson Valley, where we wrote a large portion of the book. We also wish to thank our cousins, Ilene Ferber and Bruce Janklow, for helping us to finalize the book's title.

We wish to thank Gabrielle Senza for her creative energy and for creating a beautiful book cover.

We wish to appreciate our Imago teachers, Harville Hendrix and Maya Kollman, who taught us the importance of listening through dialogue.

Special thanks to our daughter, Allison Lichter, who read numerous versions of the book, generously helped us with her editorial talent, and encouraged us to keep on writing and to complete the book.

And a deep thanks to our parents, Martha and Al Grosser and Hannah and Mike Nadler, who are no longer with us, and yet we still feel their love.

INTRODUCTION

◇◇◇◇◇◇◇◇◇◇◇◇◇◇◇◇◇◇◇◇◇◇◇◇◇◇◇◇◇◇◇◇◇◇

There is nothing more powerful in the universe than the energy of love. The purpose of this book is to inspire you with tools and real-life couples' stories to love fully. Through our own personal experience and thirty years of working with people in therapy, we know that we can grow our ability to love when we have a strong intention to connect and love and we have the tools to change old patterns of thinking and behaving. These things—the intention to love, the willingness to change, and using the tools— constitute the art of a conscious, compassionate, and loving relationship.

We've worked with people with closed hearts who have learned to trust, with recovering alcoholics who have committed themselves to becoming responsible to their partners, with co-dependents who have learned to speak their needs directly and responsibly, and with angry people who've learned to treat their partners with kindness and respect. Most of the couples who come to us, often in crisis, genuinely love their partners but don't yet have the skills and support to grow their relationship in a nourishing and healthy way.

We offer simple, powerful tools that you can use

effectively in the most difficult of situations, and that are adapted to our stressful times. We call our tools "heart tools" because they help you to discipline your mind and emotions so you can open your heart and love more. Our approach focuses on using the day-to-day encounters with your partner as opportunities to evolve into a more compassionate and loving human being and to deepen intimacy. When we consciously choose to love in any moment, we are opening our hearts. Your relationship itself becomes a path for personal growth and evolution.

We want to clarify our definitions of "heart" and "tool." By "heart" we mean the energetic heart, as well as the physical and emotional/mental powers of the heart. We use the word "tool" in the sense of the word "instrument." Just as a violin is an instrument to make music, a surgeon's scalpel is used in surgery, and a trowel is used in gardening, a tool is only as effective as the skill and the intention of the person using it. The more practice and experience the person has with the tool, the better the outcome. The same is true of the tools we offer. They need to be practiced over and over with the intention to connect and love. To support the effectiveness of our heart tools, our book offers experiential "practices" for all of the heart tools.

The techniques and practices in the book are encompassed in Compassionate Relationship Training, a course for couples that we've developed over the last ten years. Just as you need tools for other endeavors in life, you need them to succeed in your intimate relationships.

The first three chapters present the fundamental

tools for a loving and compassionate relationship: Presence, Appreciation, and Listening (PAL). The remaining chapters of the book address specific challenges that couples face and offer more heart tools that will allow you to move through difficult places by changing your thoughts and behaviors. We give you ways to change your awareness and shift your energy to respond to your loved one with more understanding and kindness.

PAL (Presence, Appreciation, and Listening) developed out of our efforts to deepen our own marriage as well as our desire to help the couples we work with. We have practiced all of the tools that we discuss in this book, and many of our clients and friends have used them effectively as well. We offer them as both inspiration and practical guidance for enhancing your relationship.

You will learn how to use the power of presence in small, everyday moments. When you go out to eat, for example, you can focus fully on being with your partner, rather than checking your e-mails or sending texts. Or when your partner comes home and asks you to listen, you can acknowledge their need and do what is possible in the moment to listen, or set a later time when you can. When you say you will show up at a certain time, you show up. If you agree to do a certain task, you follow through.

Naturally, some heart tools will work better for you than others. But before you decide which approaches work best for you and your relationship, give yourself a chance to try out all of them. If you practice them on a regular basis, they will help you to create more love in your relationship. Like any other skill, the more you practice the more competent and confident you will become. Anyone who has ever learned to play an instrument or a sport knows that it takes time and practice to become proficient.

Few of us know how to deal well with conflict. A major focus of this book is giving you tools to hang in there and learn how to transform the inevitable power struggles that arise in intimate relationships.

By practicing using these heart tools, you can bring your love to a level of satisfaction and intimacy you may never have even imagined. Beyond getting along better and reducing conflict, living consciously and cultivating the art of a compassionate and loving relationship has a wider purpose—to create more love and joy in your life, and in our world.

OUR STORY

◇◇◇◇◇◇◇◇◇◇◇◇◇◇◇◇◇◇◇◇◇◇◇◇◇◇◇◇◇◇◇◇

Both of us grew up with parents who were good people but lacked the tools to sustain and express the love they felt for each other. They didn't know how to deal with their hurts and disappointments without blaming and hurting each other. Our motivation for helping couples grows out of the pain from our own upbringings, and our desire to love to our greatest ability and to help others do so.

When we met, both of us were in our thirties, had been married before, and been single for a few years. At the time we met, Ani's son was twelve and her daughter was eight. Bill did not have children. When we introduced ourselves to each other at a friend's wedding, the attraction was immediate and strong. Bill was drawn to Ani's warmth, physical beauty, nurturing qualities, stability, and her excitement for life and spirituality. Ani was attracted to Bill's sexy good looks and his enthusiasm, heartfelt warmth, kindness and playfulness. She liked his ease in talking about his feelings, and his ability to draw her out. We lived in different states at the time—New York and New Jersey—so we began to drive back and forth on weekends to see one another. The more we came to know each other, the closer we became.

Then, two years into the relationship, we faced a crisis. Ani brought up her need to take the next step—a commitment to live together. Bill wasn't sure he was ready. Our fears, anxieties, and differences came to the fore. We argued. We even talked about breaking up.

As much as we loved each other, our escalating fear and hurt got us stuck. When he was scared, Bill called the whole relationship into question, which threatened Ani, who would withdraw to protect herself. Bill wasn't quite ready to give up his private practice and move to another state. His life blueprint was to be in private practice in New Jersey, and to be with a woman who did not have children. He was afraid he'd lose himself and give up his individual needs. He didn't have the tools to deal with his fears of not getting his needs met, without getting angry or blaming.

Ani's issues were different. Anger was an emotion she denied because she didn't have skills to deal with conflict. She didn't believe that she could express her hurt, frustration, and anger and still be loved. In an attempt to control the situation she put up with too much, hoping that her tolerance would calm Bill's reactivity. When it didn't, she pulled back emotionally and withdrew. She had to learn tools to get in touch with her anger and frustration and express those feelings, so that she could stay connected to Bill, let him know how he was affecting her, and trust him enough to deal with her feelings.

What finally helped us? We knew we loved each other and that the energy of our love was much bigger than our personal struggles. We didn't have many tools, but we had the willingness. Our commitment to make it work was reinforced by the many loving and intimate times we had shared. Once we decided to make our relationship a priority, we got help in a variety of ways: couples and communications workshops, yoga and meditation, individual psychotherapy, and training as Imago Relationship therapists. The tools we offer you today have emerged from all of these experiences.

We learned that difficulties are normal and that every couple faces a struggle of wills. That doesn't mean something is wrong with the relationship. We learned that our relationship was offering us a chance to become authentic grown-ups. We discovered that when we felt safe, we could dip into the places that we formerly tried to keep hidden because of embarrassment or shame. We recognized that we were attached to self-images that didn't reflect the whole of who we were. For example, early in our relationship when we sought help from a couples' therapist, each of us worked hard to convince the therapist that *"I'm* the nicer person!" We laugh about that now, having accepted that as "nice" as we may be, both of us harbor not-so-nice places in us, too. We accepted our humanness.

In short, we experienced how our relationship could bring up a vast ocean of self that we had been truly unconscious of. Unknown parts would suddenly pop out, like the way Ani can complain with her mother's voice, or the way Bill can try to exert control like his father. In a supportive, loving, safe relationship, more parts of ourselves can show up, and then we can make conscious choices about them. With all due respect, Dr. Freud, we see an intimate relationship on a par with the royal road of dreams as a route to the unconscious. And with all due respect to you, dear Buddha, an intimate romantic relationship with another person can be a path of transformation.

One of the exciting things about a growing relationship is discovering new things about your partner. Think of a garden—how it changes each year, and how long it takes for the plants to come into the glory of their maturity. You learn what flourishes, what might need to be moved, what needs to be fertilized, and what needs to be plucked out. That's the beauty of tending a garden: it's full of lessons, mystery, and magic!

It is the same in a relationship. If you allow for the mystery and the unknown, a relationship can grow into something magical and beautiful. But we need skills and knowledge to allow it to fully bloom. When we feel stuck in our relationship and don't know what to do, it's vital to have heart tools that can guide us out of a tough place and back on to a path of love and compassion. The tools in this book will help you to become more aware of how to be more truly intimate with your partner. Consciousness is freedom. It allows us to live from our true state of being.

first heart tool:

PRESENCE

◇◇◇◇◇◇◇◇◇◇◇◇◇◇◇◇◇◇◇◇◇◇◇◇◇

When someone is fully present, his or her
energy field radiates aliveness
and an openness to life.

—*Bill Grosser & Ani
Nadler Grosser*

In our virtual world, where so many of our relationships are mediated by a screen, we are more and more starved for real presence. As a culture, we undervalue our need for presence, and yet it is what we crave the most.

The first heart tool is Presence. What is presence? We define presence as giving our full attention to whatever we are experiencing in the moment, exactly as it is, whether painful or pleasant. When we give our full attention to the moment, we are showing up. We experience our aliveness and essential wholeness in that moment. In every fiber of our being we know we exist. Presence is a form of love.

Presence is also our true nature. We experience

it when we look into the eyes of a newborn or into the eyes of a partner in a loving moment, or when we are with someone who is dying, or when we are with a genuine spiritual teacher. Being with a pet or being immersed in nature can also be intense experiences of presence.

Will and Sandy signed up for one of our Compassionate Relationship Training workshops because they'd grown distant and felt like strangers with each other. Together since their late teens, they were now in their mid-forties, had five children, and worked hard on a small family farm. In the workshop, they particularly related to the topic of presence. Will shared that when he came home at the end of the day, Sandy was busy cooking dinner with her back to him as he came in the door. She didn't turn around to say hello, and that made him feel like he didn't exist to her. Sandy had no idea how her behavior was affecting her husband. Becoming aware of the simple act of acknowledging one another's presence was an important awareness they received, which went a long way to helping them reestablish connection.

Presence encompasses the physical, mental/ emotional, and spiritual dimensions of self. In this chapter, we offer you different doorways and practices to enter the energy of presence. Each of us has particular channels through which we enter into our aliveness. Some of us are predominantly visual, and experience the life force through images, and seeing and creating beauty. Others are more kinesthetic and feel the life force most strongly in our bodies, such as when we exercise, dance, or make love. Still others experience a special aliveness in talking or through contemplation, prayer, or meditation. Other doorways include sharing feelings, engaging in the world of ideas, hearing or making music or singing, or performing acts of generosity and kindness. All are portals to presence. Through any or all of these doorways, you can experience a powerful, in-the-moment connection to your life force and to the unity of all life.

Isabelle came in with her husband Charlie, distraught because she felt he abandoned her at a critical time. She was in a rage because he "should have known better." Charlie was stunned and defensive; he didn't think he'd done anything wrong. Isabelle told us that last week their twelve-year-old son had been in a hockey accident at school and was rushed to the hospital. She went to the hospital and called Charlie, who joined her as quickly as he could. Their son was being evaluated for a head injury, undergoing multiple tests. Since it seemed they were going to have to wait a considerable amount of time, Charlie asked Isabelle if it was okay for him to run errands. She said yes. Yet, when he didn't come back for an hour and a half, and she sat alone with no word from the medical staff about her son's status, she freaked out and became aware of her aloneness and need for her husband's support. Charlie kept maintaining his innocence: "You said it was okay for me to go, and you didn't call me either." In the session, we helped Charlie to simply be present to Isabelle's anger and fear and to her need for his physical and emotional presence in the waiting room. We helped Isabelle look at how she dismissed and devalued her need for his presence by telling herself, "I'm being irrational. I shouldn't be upset with him not being here since I told him it was okay to leave." The session helped both of them to realize that sometimes the most important thing we can give is simply to be there for the other. Charlie and Isabelle began to value interconnection, and the truth that we need support and the other's presence, especially when we are in a crisis and scared.

Presence is powerful: you know it when you experience it. When you meet someone for the first time, you know within seconds whether or not they are present. You feel connected to them—or not. When someone is fully present, his or her energy field radiates aliveness and an openness to life. They may be quiet and unassuming in their personalities, but we sense they are connected to the larger field of life.

The state of being physically present sets the tone for the immediate response we get from another person. If you show up with your partner and you are totally "there," not multitasking but fully attentive to your partner, then you are entirely physically present with your loved one. This is crucial to deepening intimacy in your life. Think back to your early months with your partner and how physically present you were then. You only wanted to be with him or her, fully and joyfully!

The other aspect of physical presence is the way you communicate with your body. Most communication is nonverbal. Are you leaning forward while you're talking, or do you angle your body back? Do you have a smile on your face or a frown? Are you standing and/or sitting straight, or are you slouched over? Are you making eye contact? Our body powerfully communicates our state of being.

Wouldn't it be attractive if you spoke to your partner with your body moving gently toward him or her and shared genuine feelings without blame or judgment? That is presence on a physical level. When we are not physically present, others notice immediately. For example, if your partner comes home while you're on the computer and you don't pause to make eye contact or say hello, you're giving a clear message that he or she is not the priority at that moment. It is not wrong to have a different focus in the moment; you can respectfully acknowledge your partner and explain that you are engaged with a task, and will be present with them at another specific time—say, in a half hour, or right after dinner. Don't try to "act" present when you're really engaged with something else. You can't fake presence.

Another essential part of physical presence is showing up when you agree to show up. We cannot overestimate the importance of reliability. It creates certainty, stability, and safety in a relationship. This is a fundamental aspect of being physically present.

The next aspect of presence is the way you think and feel—your mental and emotional states. These states are strong, initial communicators to another person and can be picked up in a millisecond. Another word to describe this aspect of presence is "attitude." It's very easy to tell immediately what kind of attitude another person has.

Is your attitude positive or negative? This often comes down to whether you are judgmental or not. Most of us find it very difficult to be nonjudgmental, since our culture actually trains us to be "critical thinkers." We are trained to prioritize our linear, cognitive "left" brain, which helps us to analyze and scrutinize. This may work well in many situations, but it can be hazardous in relationships. If your intention is to become more intimate with your partner, judgment and scrutiny will only get in the way. If we focus on what's wrong with our partner, that "wrongness" will become our reality. When we focus on loving thoughts and feelings towards our partner, we feel more love within ourselves and towards our partner.

What do we do with critical and unloving thoughts towards our partner? We are not saints. The truth is we don't always feel positive and loving; many things about our partner trigger us. To grow our relationship, we have to acknowledge pain and problems and not deny them. For example, if we feel ignored by our partner, we need to acknowledge that this bothers us, rather than pretend it doesn't, and communicate what bothers us without blame. Otherwise, we might lash out or withdraw and never get to the real issues.

We have created the N.O.W. principle as a way to remember important aspects of emotional and mental presence. The N.O.W. principle allows you to stay in connection, no matter what the circumstances. It is a practice to stay engaged. The N.O.W. principle encompasses **N**ot judging the other person, remaining **O**pen, and **W**elcoming differences. More specifically:

Not judging means that you take responsibility that it is your critical mind that is creating the judgments. It's your reaction and your choice about how to deal with your judgments. Let's say, for example, that you're out to dinner with your partner and he or

6

she repeatedly interrupts you as you're talking. You become irritated and say to yourself, "There she goes again, always interrupting me. She's so self-centered!" First, acknowledge to yourself that you are judging and that your feeling is of irritation. Then, decide what's most important to you this evening—is it stewing about your partner's annoying characteristics or is it enjoying this time together? If it's the latter, you may want to say, "I really want to be with you, and it's hard for me to be with you when you keep interrupting. I'd like you to hear what I have to say, too." You are trying to handle your experience without being critical, while at the same time respecting your own feelings and needs.

Being **O**pen is another form of presence, and it is a conscious decision to be with another person and be in the experience with them as it is. At any given moment, you or your partner may be angry, happy, or preoccupied. Being open does not mean you have to like how you or your partner is feeling. Being open honors feelings, and it also honors that we have different feelings at the same time.

Welcoming differences means that you are acknowledging that you and your partner are separate people. Your partner has his or her distinctive way of seeing the world, and so do you. Your partner's perceptions, thoughts, feelings, sensations, and other experiences are different from yours. Neither of you is "right" or "wrong"—just different.

Dealing with differences is challenging when we are under stress, especially when we imagine that our partner is thinking and feeling differently than we do. We humans tend to want others to think like we do because of our need for predictability and security. Because this is a challenge for most couples, we go into this in more depth in the next chapter, and we want to give an example right now.

Jana and Mark came from very different cultural backgrounds and had different ideas about what was safe for their one-year-old baby. In a session with them, Jana explained that it is very important to her that people take off their shoes before entering their apartment so that the baby would not pick up any germs. Mark agreed to this, even though it was not so important to him. They got into a big fight after their daughter's first birthday party because one of Mark's friends didn't take off his shoes and walked right onto the rug where the baby was playing. Jana was furious at Mark for not insisting that his friend take off his shoes, and she accused him of putting the baby's health in jeopardy. Their differences about safety were highlighted. Mark said, "What's the big deal? Babies have to get used to germs." The more he forced his point of view on her, the more she felt unheard and got angrier. We asked her if she thought that Mark was a protective father. She acknowledged that he is indeed a good and protective father and takes care of the baby's safety. This bigger perspective helped her relax. He was able to be present with her as she expressed her anxiety about keeping the baby safe. His understanding deepened as she talked about the high infant mortality rate in the country where she grew up. They were able to work together to have a plan for dealing with the shoes the next time they had guests. When we make room for our partner to be a separate person from us, we create a space for an open and loving relationship.

In this chapter, we talked about the different doorways to presence. When we are connected from a place of aliveness in ourselves, we have the opportunity to experience our partner and the whole world as manifestations of the same glorious energy. This is what we most crave—to be in connection with ourselves, others, and life itself.

Practices for Presence

What follows are many practices that have helped us develop presence in our lives. We encourage you to take the time to try out these powerful practices.

INTENTIONALLY MAKING CONTACT

You and your partner stand directly facing each other for one minute. Look into each other's eyes. Take several breaths into your heart, letting your chest relax. You are intentionally making contact. You're fully there for your partner. As you do this, your energy will begin to infuse your partner's body, and his/hers will begin to permeate yours. Smell, taste, touch, see, feel, and hear the essence of each other's energy. This is a direct experience of physical presence. When you first try this exercise, it may feel awkward or "too intense." This makes sense; you are tapping into a vast, powerful energy field, and you may not be used to so much intensity. Stay with it. In time, you will become more comfortable. This exercise will help you feel closer and more engaged with your partner.

SLOWING DOWN

This practice involves taking a moment to consciously slow down when you are with your partner. We practiced this just the other day. We were each getting ready to go into our respective offices to meet with clients. We stopped and looked at each other, and then gave each other a long hug. The whole experience lasted only about twenty seconds, but we slowed ourselves down enough to feel the presence of the other. In this precious and delicious, here-and-now moment, we were utterly delighted to be with each other. And the glow still lingers!

THE THREE BREATH TECHNIQUE

Under stress, our breath becomes contracted and shallow. We get tense and go into a fight, flight, or freeze response. That is we try to protect ourselves by lashing out, running away, or remaining in the situation but "freezing" our emotions. When we shut off thoughts, feelings, and energy from ourselves and the other person, we lose what we most want— to be connected. The Three Breath Technique helps us to stay open, connected, and present, so that we don't go into a stress response.

Try this right now: *Breathe in while counting to five and then exhale for five counts. Breathe in the rhythm that is natural to you in this moment. Focus on the bodily sensations of breathing in for the entire inhale and on the bodily sensations of the breath flowing out for the entire exhale. It helps if you focus on where you feel the sensation of breath* *most strongly, such as the nostrils, chest, belly, or fingertips. Take a moment to notice where you feel your breath most strongly right now. You don't have to change your breathing pattern; just stay with it as it is in this moment. Repeat this conscious breathing exercise at least three times.*

Being conscious of your breath allows you to lower reactivity so you can be more present. You can try it anytime you feel uncomfortable. This simple practice can help you to be in the moment in a fuller, more peaceful way. You can also use it whenever you want to intensify your feelings of aliveness and pleasure.

OPENNESS TO PRESENT-MOMENT EXPERIENCE

When you're in a good mood and walk into a room where you perceive your partner as being mad, first notice your own reactions by tuning into your body, your thinking, and your emotions. Are you tightening up and holding your breath? Notice your thoughts and feelings: Are you thinking "it's my fault" or judging "here he/she goes again, always having a problem?" You may need to first take a breath and relax and attend to the reactive part of yourself.

Then you can ask your partner in a neutral and even curious way, "How are you and can I be of help?" Approaching another person in a state of presence is like imagining that your arms are open rather than tightly closed across your chest, and holding that other person away from you.

GUIDED IMAGERY: IMAGINING CONNECTION

Often, we wait for our partner to create a loving and peaceful state of being between us. We may be tired, depressed, or anxious and want our partner to take the first step in helping to change our mood. And it is true that if our partner is in a positive state of mind, his or her good cheer may change our mood, which in turn will help us to feel more positive and loving.

But we can also change our emotional state ourselves by shifting our focus. We need to first be conscious that we are choosing to change our mindset. Once we make that choice, we can move on to use the guided imagery of Imagining Connection.

First read the entire practice, and then put down the book and let yourself experience the imagery. You can also record the imagery, and play it back:

Think of the most loving moment you have enjoyed with your partner in recent months. Perhaps you were at the beach together, or making love, or having an intimate conversation. Take a moment and think of that loving experience. Be aware of what feelings come up as you think about it. Be aware of what part of your body is re-experiencing the feeling. Is it your heart, belly, arms, legs, face, or other parts of the body? As you begin to feel the experience of this loving moment with your partner, notice how your reality changes. Whenever you encounter a difficult experience with your partner, you can think back to this loving experience, and return to a state of calm, grounded mental/emotional presence.

GUIDED IMAGERY: DOING WHAT YOU LOVE

Think of something that is important to you at this moment in your life. For example, if you feel particularly alive in nature, you can sense that calling inside of you and go outside. You might take a walk, rake leaves, look at the sky, watch the moving clouds, see the stars. If you enjoy music, listen to your favorite music. Let yourself fully experience what you love, within your body. This puts you in a positive state and helps you be more present with your partner.

GUIDED IMAGERY: LIVING FROM YOUR HEART

Another way to experience presence is to live from your heart. Our deepest truth lives in our heart center. Our heart is the seat of the soul, and it is powerful and wise beyond compare. In the yogic tradition, the heart chakra (energy center in the subtle body) relates to balance, love, compassion, and relationship. To survive as a species, humans must learn to live from the heart. Anodea Judith is an internationally known expert on the chakra system. Her newest book, *The Global Heart Awakens*, is a powerful call to humanity to live from the heart.

Science is beginning to recognize what the masters of all spiritual traditions have always known about the importance of the heart. In the last twenty years, the Institute for Heart Math has been studying the intelligence of the heart, what they call "the heart brain." They've measured that the electromagnetic field of the heart is many times greater than that of the brain. They also discuss the role the heart plays in hormonal regulation, including the production of oxytocin, the bonding hormone, which is of particular relevance to intimate relationships. We encourage you to look at their website to help you better understand the power of the heart tools we present in this book.

To develop the habit of living from your heart, try this exercise below. First read the entire practice, and then put down the book and let yourself experience the imagery. You can also record the imagery, and play it back.

Place your hand on your heart to focus your awareness at the heart. Consciously relax and soften the muscles in the chest wall. Imagine breathing in and out of the center of your chest. Breathe in to the count of five and breathe out to the count of five. Imagine a safe place where you can relax. It could be in the mountains, the beach, or sitting in a comfortable chair in your living room. Take a moment to experience being in this peaceful place.

Now, think of a moment in your life when you felt loved. The love may have come from a parent, a partner, a child, a pet, a friend, a teacher, a grandparent, or other relative. Feel the breath carrying the energy of the love, and feel it in your heart, as it fills and spreads through your entire being.

When you focus on your heart, your mind naturally slows down, and you get in touch with what really matters to you. You focus on what is truly important to you. The byproduct of listening to your heart is that it quiets the fearful, anxious chatter of your mind. When you are connected to your heart, you are always in the present moment. You lower your emotional reactivity and give yourself more choices about how to handle a situation. You develop the "observer" inside you. This is the part of your mind that is aware of your thoughts, feelings, and sensations and knows that they are not fixed structures but come and go. The observer is like the beam of light from a lighthouse that illuminates everything it touches. You can think of the observer as the larger mind, the part that has a wider perspective. We can train this capacity through mindfulness and meditation.

Living from our hearts not only allows us to experience a mind-body connection within ourselves but also a connection to other beings and to a universal Self. This opens us up to a wider picture of how we can be in the world. We learn to live from the reality of how we are all interconnected, rather than from the illusion of separation. We begin to focus not only on what we want to give ourselves, but also on what we want to give others. That is expansive. We have so much to give when we get out of our own way.

GUIDED IMAGERY:
REMEMBERING THE CHILD IN YOU

Another way to live from your heart is to remember what made you feel alive as a child. When we touch that lively, spirited place, we are in the present moment. It might be going to the park, jumping on a bike, playing with friends, reading, sitting in church or synagogue, or playing in the street. For Bill, feeling alive as a child was playing in the park, swinging on the swings, and especially playing baseball. For Ani, it was riding on her bike, dashing downhill, and taking her hands off the handlebars: "Look Ma, no hands!" Ani also felt very alive when she laughed and giggled with her girlfriends.

First read the entire practice, and then put down the book and let yourself experience the imagery. You can also record the imagery, and play it back.

Find a comfortable, quiet place where you can relax. Take some breaths in and out, feeling your breath move through your body. Now, think of a place where you went as a child that was your magical place, where you felt safe and protected no matter what was going on around you. It might have been swinging on a swing in the park, or sitting under a favorite tree or in a comfy chair you could sink into and read uninterruptedly. Notice what you see around you. Notice the sounds and smells. Let yourself fully experience what it is like to be in this safe, protected space.

Now, take some time to think about what made you feel most alive as a child. Notice what you are doing in your special place. Are you running, skipping, drawing, imagining, singing, playing, or reading? Let yourself experience the aliveness in your body. Because the body remembers, you can return to this experience any time and deeply feel your essential aliveness.

To foster emotional intimacy, we encourage you to share your imagery with your partner.

second heart tool:

APPRECIATION

∞∞∞∞∞∞∞∞∞∞∞∞∞∞∞∞∞∞∞∞∞∞∞

Those tender words we said to one another are
stored in the secret heart of heaven. One day, like the rain,
they will fall and spread. And their mystery
will grow green over the world.

—Rumi

In this chapter, we discuss how appreciation plays a key part in changing the consciousness of a relationship. Appreciation is our second heart tool.

Appreciations are positive messages that you think about and/or express toward another person. It may be an appreciation for something they've done, something they've said, or for who they are in the world. Simply thinking about appreciations in your mind changes your brain chemistry, and you'll find yourself with a more positive and loving attitude.

Nonetheless, it is also very important to directly express the appreciation you feel for your partner. Many of us appreciate a lot about our loved ones, but don't make it a point to tell them. All of us want to know we are appreciated. We want to appreciate the originators of Imago Relationship Therapy, Harville Hendrix and Helen LaKelly Hunt, for the emphasis they put in our training on the importance of sharing appreciations and of eliminating negativity in your relationship.

Claire and Roger were a couple we worked with who frequently exchanged critical, nasty remarks. These exchanges often escalated into fierce fights. Then, in a therapy session, we gave them a homework assignment to say three appreciations every day.

"No!" they protested instantly and in unison, offering many practical reasons why it would be impossible. They worked different shifts and Claire was sleeping while Roger was working. However, they did want to be more loving and passionate with each other—that's why they'd come to therapy in the first place. So, somewhat reluctantly, they took on the homework.

In short order, they became quite creative about their assignment. Each morning when Roger got up for work, he wrote three appreciations on a sticky note and put it inside the pantry door where the couple kept their coffee cups. Then, later in the day, when Claire returned from her second shift, she left appreciations for Roger in the pantry as well. Each day, each person received three appreciations from the other, in addition to all of the accumulated appreciations from past days that were still posted in the pantry.

This explosion of loving gestures from partner to partner dramatically changed the way Claire and Roger related to each other. They moved from being highly critical and angry to being friendlier and more responsive. Instead of yelling, they started to listen to each other when they were upset, which gave them more possibilities for resolving difficulties.

Habits are powerful: If you build up years and years of resentment, then you will inevitably focus on negativity. But the opposite is true as well. By focusing on the things you love about your partner, you will experience more positive and loving feelings towards him or her. Appreciation wakes you up to your own positive feelings towards your partner, and sharing them will feel like striking gold—to both of you.

In our work with Darlene and Jack, Darlene was surprised that Jack repeatedly shared how much he appreciated the lunches she made for him to take to work. For her this seemed trivial, and initially she reacted with a judgment: "Is *that* all you appreciate about me?" But one evening, as he once again expressed this appreciation, Jack became aware of why this was important to him. He shared with Darlene that he'd grown up with a single mom, who had to run out to work every morning and never had time to pack his lunch. It made him feel deeply cared for that Darlene took the time to pack him a tasty and filling lunch.

In the same session, Darlene appreciated that when Jack came home from work the evening before, he had asked how her day went and was sincerely interested in what she had to say. This meant a lot to Darlene, because she had grown up as a middle child with eight siblings. Her parents were so busy working and keeping track of basic needs that they never had time to ask the children how their day went.

As with this couple, we have found that an appreciation often has a deeper meaning that both partners can enjoy discovering. In this way, appreciations are like treasure chests. Appreciations keep our hearts open, allowing them to expand, like accordions.

The Power of Appreciation

A loving act on your part, no matter how small, will begin to feed your relationship. Our friend Matt told us how his feelings of appreciation for his wife, Julie, transformed a dynamic in their relationship that used to create conflict. He told us he'd cut a business trip short to come home and help Julie after a power surge had destroyed her computer. "I'm coming home to be with you," he told her on the phone.

This was not his usual response. Typically, he would have told her to call a repair person, or he would try to coach her on the phone to fix it herself. Matt had grown up with undemonstrative, highly logical parents who rarely expressed positive emotions and affection. He didn't have role models for tuning in emotionally and extending himself to another person.

Julie said she was delighted that Matt had responded so sensitively to her emotional distress, rather than to just see it as a practical problem. It meant a lot to her that he actually extended himself by coming home. When we asked Matt what prompted this new behavior, he remembered that just the day before, he'd been deeply appreciating having Julie in his life. He'd felt his whole body fill with love for her. He told us that he suspected that these overwhelmingly loving feelings must have overridden his habitual "fix-it" responses, which usually ignored the emotional needs of his wife.

Appreciations communicate to your partner what's important to you. For example, Jane told her husband Sam: "I really appreciate that you took the kids to school because I was overloaded with work responsibilities and you freed me up to get some of that work done. That meant a lot to me." Among other things, she was telling Sam that it is important to her that he values her work and was willing to lighten her load so she could attend to it. When you think of appreciation as a form of love, each word or act of gratitude that you express helps you to create a necklace of love in your life. You begin to view your partner in a very positive, compassionate way—as a precious jewel in your necklace rather than a burden around your neck. Moment to moment, we can choose to do this in a conscious, loving way.

Appreciating the Effort

It is important to appreciate your partner when he or she is making an effort on your behalf. Appreciation of this kind instills hope. A partner's efforts can come in many different forms—listening more attentively, being less critical, expressing compliments, being more relaxed around you, making more time to be with you, or doing chores without being asked. When you notice these kinds of efforts, absolutely let your partner know. Watch your relationship begin to blossom.

The Hazards of Negativity

So much of our frustration, anger, and contempt arise when we assume that our partner can't change. We imagine that our partner doesn't care enough about us to understand, listen, or appreciate us. The belief that they "just don't care" gets fixed in our minds. We create a negative story about them. And when we fail to acknowledge their positive efforts, and continue to assume that they don't care, they start to act that way. By contrast, when we notice that our partner is making efforts, even if they're small ones, and we communicate our appreciation, it can create an upward spiral of renewed love.

It's very easy to be critical of one's partner. It is human nature that we won't like everything our partner does. However, it is another thing to focus large amounts of energy on what frustrates or annoys us about him or her. This can become an obsession that keeps us distant from our loved one. The bottom line: chronic negativity will never bring you closer to your partner.

Practices for Appreciation

A DAILY PRACTICE

Why do we emphasize appreciation so much? Because it can truly transform your relationship. Studies by psychologists John and Julie Gottman show that for every negative message you have given your partner, you need to give at least *five* positive messages to emerge with a positive balance. By giving a positive message—in this case, an appreciation—each day to your partner, you create openness and positive energy for both of you.

There are two elements of a daily appreciation. The first part is privately reflecting on what you appreciate about your partner, and the second part is expressing it. To illustrate: At the beginning of most of our therapy sessions, we invite couples to take a few breaths to slow down and to reflect on something they appreciate about their partner. The appreciation can be something about their partner's character or a small act of thoughtfulness that comes to mind in the moment. We tell couples it's OK to repeat the same appreciations.

SHARING APPRECIATIONS

This practice can take as little as five minutes. It uses the mirroring process we learned in our Imago Relationship Therapy Training.

Sit down, across from each other, so you are making eye contact. Become present with the Three Breath Technique, a practice used with the heart tool of Presence. One partner begins by sharing his/her appreciation. The other mirrors back the words and energy of the appreciation starting with "what I heard you say is..." The partner who is sharing nods to acknowledge that his/her appreciation was accurately received. If it was not fully received, they can share it again. They may also want to share a little more, such as why the particular appreciation was important to them. This is not about analysis but simply sharing why they were touched, as you saw in the appreciation between Darlene and Jack. Then you switch, and the listening partner shares his/her appreciation, and the other partner mirrors back.

GREETINGS

How do you greet your partner first thing in the morning, during the day when you leave and come home, and just before bedtime? In the morning, do you say "hello" with positive energy, or do you bark out a list of chores that need to be done that day? In the evening, do you return home from work tense and hunched over, drop your briefcase on the floor and silently walk into another room? Or, if you are the one at home, do you "greet" your partner when he/she arrives home by complaining about everything that has gone wrong that day?

Kayla, a client of ours, recently told us that she arrived at a party before her husband, Jeff, had shown up. When he arrived a half hour later, he extended a general "hello" to everyone, looking affably around the room. This was a delicate time in their relationship: Kayla and Jeff were recovering from Jeff's affair. In their next couple's session, she expressed how much she would have liked it if he had first made a beeline to her and greeted her warmly with a kiss. Kayla wanted to know she was special to Jeff. Fortunately, he was able to hear this as a request, not as a criticism.

Each morning, the two of us make it a point to lovingly greet each other. When we leave the house, we say goodbye in a pleasant way, making eye contact and maybe exchanging a hug and kiss. When we can't do this in person, the first one to leave leaves a playful and loving note on the kitchen counter. This practice makes each of us feel valued.

Nightly greetings are important, too. Before going to bed each evening, remember to say goodnight to your partner in a warm and pleasant way. Greetings are an important part of showing love throughout the day.

HUGS

We recommend that you make loving physical contact with your partner every day. You can choose any number of ways to do this—an arm around the shoulder, a gentle hand on the back or, best of all, a warm hug. When we see couples for counseling and in workshops, we suggest that they hug at least three times a day. And we mean a long hug, not a cursory one.

Over and over again, we hear from couples how vital hugging and touching are to re-establishing and solidifying their emotional connection. Hugging reduces stress and boosts our levels of endorphins and oxytocin, the bonding hormone.

All of these practices can help you to become closer and more loving with your partner. Requiring only a few minutes each day, they open up your mind, heart, body, and spirit.

third heart tool:

COMPASSIONATE LISTENING

<><><><><><><><><><><><><><><><><><><><><><><><><><><><><><><><>

Listen as if you cannot always tell what the truth is.
Listen as if you might be wrong, especially when you are
convinced you are right. Listen as if you are willing to
take the risk of going beyond your righteousness.
Listen as if love mattered.

—*Kelly Tobey*

Betsey was chronically irritated with her husband, Rick, because he went to the gym nearly every day after work, sometimes not returning home until 8 p.m. Betsey thought this amount of exercise was excessive and hazardous to Rick's overall health, even if it was good for his heart. Also, she missed her husband. "Why do you have to go *now*? You'd rather be at the gym than be with me," she complained.

Usually, Rick said little in response. But one afternoon, in the middle of a therapy session, he exploded. "What the hell do you *want* from me?" he shouted. With our help, the couple used the opportunity of Rick's intense reaction to begin to talk about this—and to really listen to each other. Listening helped Betsey understand that for Rick, exercising was a physical and emotional release as well as an important way to maintain his cardiac health since his heart surgery two years ago. Because Betsey was able to truly listen to Rick's point of view, and understand that he was not rejecting her, she began to relax and let go of her fear-based judgments. She also was able to articulate that she desired more time with him and Rick was open to hearing her needs when she expressed them without blame. As a result of these exchanges, the couple decided to set aside a regular date night once a week. Before long, they began to feel closer.

Listening is an enormously compassionate act and is our third heart tool. The more that we take the time to understand what our partner is telling us, the more deeply we can appreciate his/her perspective on life. It is important to accept that your partner has a different way of seeing the world. It isn't that their perspective or your perspective is right or wrong. They are just different. One of the major difficulties that couples face is failing to take the time to listen to each other in order to deeply understand the other's perspective.

It is not uncommon for partners to complain to one another periodically about something—and then just drop it. They try to avoid the issue because it's too uncomfortable, and they don't know how to talk about uncomfortable things. They may feel that their partner won't be able to openly and actively listen to them. But think about it this way: It will upset your partner much more if you eventually turn your back on the relationship without addressing what's bothering you. Give your partner a chance to work with you to resolve the issues.

The FAR Principle

The "FAR" principle, as we call it, is grounded in the belief that when partners listen to each other, they don't need to **F**ix anything, they don't have to **A**gree, and they don't have to be **R**ight. Let's explore each of these concepts in turn:

You don't need to Fix anything. This is where men, especially, get into trouble. Many men tend to jump in with a logical, problem-solving response because they want to take away their partner's distress. They may be uncomfortable with their partner's emotional distress or feel it is their role to be "the fixer."

In fact, when you listen to another person, you don't have to fix anything. It's often a very bad idea to try. When your partner is talking about feelings, it may be very annoying to him or her to have you try to "solve" them, even if a practical problem is attached to the feelings. A good way to check this out is to directly ask your partner whether she/he wants you to offer a practical solution. You can ask: "Would you like me to give you my take on this or would you prefer I just listen?" That way, you are giving your partner an opportunity to say, "No, I only want you to listen to me," or, "Yes, I would like your ideas."

You don't have to Agree. Another key aspect of listening is that you don't have to agree with your partner as long you are making an effort to understand what he/she is saying. As a matter of fact, you don't have to agree with a lot of things that your partner says. It may be easier if you agree, but it's not a necessity, and it never happens all the time between two individuals. What is important is that you take the time to try to understand the other person.

You don't have to be Right. When we work with couples, the first thing we teach them is that each partner has a different perspective, and that understanding the other's perspective will help partners to find a way toward greater closeness. When we don't feel listened to, it's very easy to become defensive and turn the discussion into a right-or-wrong battle. The moment we begin to justify our "rightness," we have temporarily lost our connection. Healthy relationships are based on mutual love and trust, not on who's right and who's wrong. We often ask couples: "Which do you prefer—to be right or to be connected?"

Listening is a way of meeting your partner halfway. We envision it as a bridge. Imagine the two of you standing on opposite sides of the bridge; as you listen to your partner and as he/she listens to you, you both begin to walk toward the center of the bridge. Listening is the process that bridges the gap between partners. Part of the beauty of listening is that it frees you from having to try so hard to figure out what your partner needs, because he or she tells you directly. For your part, you are giving your partner a great gift by fully, compassionately listening to what matters to him or her.

The Rhythm of Relationship

Relationships are like accordions, pulsating in and out. Sometimes there is more closeness and intimacy, while other times there is less. This is a natural process in a relationship. What is important is establishing a balance between intimacy with a partner and time alone as an individual. A healthy relationship makes room for both.

Every relationship has an inner rhythm. There is a time to talk about issues and a time *not* to talk about them. When you and your partner have agreed to talk about an issue, that is the time to talk. When one person is not ready—too upset, too angry, or too tired—that is not the time to talk. It just won't work. Sometimes, when the first partner is anxious to talk *now* and the second partner doesn't want to, the first partner will pressure the other to have a discussion. When this occurs, the second partner may simply shut down which, in turn, is apt to make the first partner more agitated.

If you're the one who wants to talk and your partner resists, ask whether he/she is willing to talk about the issue at some other point in the near future. Be sure to ask this question in a respectful, calm, nonjudgmental way. If your partner is indeed willing to talk at another point, he or she can simply say, "Yes, but not now," and then offer another, better time to talk about the issue. This gives your partner a meaningful choice in the matter, while also keeping you from feeling pushed aside. You now know that there will be another discussion, and that you will soon be heard.

In a situation in which one partner refuses to talk about an issue and declares that he/she *never* wants to talk about it, what can you do? First, you can simply ask, "Help me understand why you don't you want to talk about it?" If your partner can't explain it because he/she really doesn't know, this may be a situation when you can say to your partner, "If we can't talk about it, maybe this is a time when we need some professional help, from a counselor or clergy person."

How *Not* to Communicate

Be aware of what factors undermine communication with your partner. For example, you may come from a background where people yell and scream frequently. To you, it may seem perfectly natural to speak loudly.

To your partner, however, it may feel like abuse. To her/him, screaming and yelling may feel like being shot in the heart. It is easy enough to dismiss one's partner as "too sensitive." But if you want to understand and be with your partner, you need to know and take seriously your impact on his/her emotional well being.

Examples of harmful communication include saying to your partner, "You're crazy!" or "You don't know what you're talking about" or "You're so mean!" They are not just words or facts; they have powerfully harsh, critical energy behind them. They're likely to leave scars on your partner. The next time you're ready to say a harsh word, we recommend that you pause and take three breaths before you say anything.

Many times, we are not aware of how strongly our negative energy affects our partner. A client named John recalls that early in his relationship with his wife, Susan, he'd raise his voice and think nothing of it. "Stop finishing my sentences for me!" he would thunder to Susan. "I can't think straight when you do that!"

Susan found his tone and energy upsetting and threatening. Once John understood this, he tried to be more mindful of his inflection. As he became more aware of what he was feeling, he could communicate anger and hurt without yelling. He was able to tell Susan, "I would like to finish what I am saying, and I would like you to stop interrupting." Later on, John could acknowledge that it hurt his feelings when she didn't give him a chance to finish speaking. When John spoke in a softer voice, Susan was finally able to understand that it was hurtful to him when she impatiently finished his sentences. She became mindful of this old habit and was able to stop it. By taking the time to understand what bothers your partner and what helps your partner feel safe, you're changing the relationship for both of you.

Just as yelling and screaming can be abusive, so can withdrawing from your partner. Another term for this is "stonewalling." The stonewalling partner may feel that he or she is just trying to reclaim a sense of safety by becoming quiet and unavailable. However, to the other partner, it may feel like neglect and abandonment. Stonewalling can up the ante, even though the withdrawing partner believes that she/he is only trying to avoid an argument. Often, the withdrawing partner is angry, and this energy gets broadcast loud and clear to the other partner.

The reality is that withdrawing can be just as painful and hurtful to your partner as loud and explosive words. There is nothing wrong with asking to take a time-out from your partner. It is another thing entirely, however, to shut down, withdraw, and not come back. The dynamic we often see with couples is that the more one partner withdraws, the more the other escalates by yelling, which creates a vicious cycle.

Partners who tend to withdraw usually are afraid of conflict and don't know how to set boundaries or take time for themselves. When their withdrawal provokes their partner to yell and argue, the withdrawing partner interprets it as justification for further stonewalling: "I've got to get out of here." The key is for the one who yells to contain his or her anger and intensity, and the one who withdraws to make a conscious effort to remain engaged. Calm, respectful engagement on both sides is a prerequisite for intimacy.

Mirroring

One of the most direct and potent listening skills is mirroring, which we use frequently with the couples we work with as well as in our own relationship. We learned this practice in our training as Imago therapists. Mirroring can be very simple, and can be a "stand-alone" practice, or part of the Imago Intentional Dialogue, which we describe later in this chapter.

To mirror: *Sit with your partner, face to face, and take turns speaking for perhaps 5 to 10 minutes about a particular issue while the other listens and mirrors back what they've heard. Then switch roles: the speaker becomes the listener, and the listener gets a chance to be the speaker.*

When you mirror, you simply reflect back what you've heard. After your partner speaks a few sentences, then you, the listener, say: "What I hear you saying is..." You can paraphrase your partner's statements or repeat them back word for word. If the speaker has a preference to be mirrored word for word, then the listener honors that preference.

Please note that, as the listener, it is important to respect your own capacity to remember. Feel free to ask your partner to pause, so you can comfortably reflect back. Mirroring is not a memory test; it is a collaborative activity to increase understanding. In addition to repeating the words as best you can, try to mirror your partner's energy, in order to sensitively communicate that you have fully heard the message. Also, it is important from time to time for the listener to ask the speaker, "Did I get it?" This gives the speaker a moment to check in with him/herself about whether they feel understood. It gives the speaker time to clarify thoughts and feelings. A great beauty of the mirroring process is that it slows us down to reflect, and this in itself lowers tension.

When we mirror, we want to communicate authentic understanding. We are not just going through the motions mechanically, parrot-like.

When we mirror, we are listening to our partner in a truly open, non-critical way. We are saying back what we hear without inserting our own subjective thoughts or "spin" on what our partner is saying. Our objective is to understand our partner from his/her viewpoint, without becoming reactive. This can be challenging when your partner is talking about an issue that is charged between you. It's all too easy to inject our own thoughts, interpretations, or ask questions. Avoid doing this, because it will interrupt the flow of the partner who is speaking.

If you are having difficulty containing your reactions, we offer several techniques you can use:

1) Imagine you are literally sitting on your thoughts/feelings/opinions and remember that you will have your turn to respond.

2) Shift your awareness into your body, feel your feet on the ground, and follow your breath until it gets steady.

3) If what your partner is sharing is very scary to you, acknowledge that to yourself internally, and comfort the scared part of yourself as a parent would comfort a small child.

In short, mirroring requires discipline and concentration. Mirroring slows down your mind to be fully present to what your partner is saying, instead of what you're thinking about and what you want to say back to him/her. When we listen in this way, our brain waves slow down the same way they do in meditation. In this way, the heart tool of Compassionate Listening is a mindfulness practice.

You can use mirroring for a variety of purposes. One is to discuss an issue that, in ordinary conversation, would produce reactivity and defensiveness. That issue might be children, money, sex, and/or extended family members. Before starting the process, you will need to agree on a topic, and agree about how long you will mirror on this topic. You may also want to agree that your goal is not a solution but rather understanding. Please don't pressure yourselves to work out everything in one sitting. Depending on the issue, it may take many dialogues to create deeper understanding, and the breaks between mirroring sessions can be useful to deepen personal understanding and perspective.

You can also use mirroring when you are not talking about a specific topic, but your partner is upset and simply wants you to listen to her/him. As the listener, you need to get your partner's permission to mirror before you begin. By reflecting back what they say, you are listening without "fixing" the problem or otherwise reacting.

Mirroring is also a wonderful tool even when the topic is not about your relationship. You or your partner may want to talk about work, dreams, hopes, worries, or politics. Mirroring helps the speaker to clarify his/her thoughts and feelings. Mirroring can be very helpful when one partner is trying to problem solve and wants to think out loud, without receiving any suggestions. We love what Brenda Ueland says about the magical and magnetic power of listening in *Tell Me More: On the Fine Art of Listening:* "When we are listened to, it creates us, makes us unfold and expand. Ideas actually begin to grow within us and come to life. You know how if a person laughs at your jokes you become funnier and funnier; and if he does not, every tiny little joke in you weakens up and dies."

The Intentional Dialogue

Through our work as Certified Imago Relationship therapists, we have learned a wonderfully effective communication tool called the Intentional Dialogue. It includes four components: Mirroring (which we just described), Summary, Validation, and Empathy.

Please note that before dialoguing, both partners need to agree to dialogue and they need to agree on the topic as well as a time frame for how long to dialogue.

Mirroring. Mirroring is the first part of the Intentional Dialogue.

Summary. When the speaking partner has finished talking, it is helpful for the listener to summarize in a few sentences the essence of what the speaker has said. This serves many purposes, including making sure you got the main points, and that you understand what your partner is saying. This gives the speaker a chance to further clarify if there is something the listener missed, or if the speaker has something to add.

Validation. The next part of the Intentional Dialogue is called "validation." When you listen and mirror back to your partner, you begin to develop a deep appreciation for your partner's perspective. Your linear, logical thinking begins to shift into an emotional understanding of your partner's perspective. Another way of saying this is that via mirroring, you move from your rational left brain to your emotional right brain. Using both sides of your brain can bring powerfully positive results.

When you validate, you convey that what your partner has said makes sense to you from *their point of view*. As the listener, you may not agree with what your partner says, and that's perfectly okay. But the more actively you listen, the more likely you'll be to truly understand your partner's perspective. At this point, you can validate your partner's reality.

Think of it this way: Your partner makes sense to himself or herself. Your job is to try to understand that "sense." Again, this does not mean you have to see it the same way.

When Delores and David were dialoguing in a session, Delores started tearing up as she told David that when he leaves without saying goodbye in the morning, "I feel as if you don't love me."

Now, that was not David's reality at all. When he initially heard Delores say this, his first reaction was to become annoyed and defensive. "You always make a mountain out of a molehill," he retorted. But the more he listened to Delores during their dialogue, the more he could understand her perspective. It made more sense later in the dialogue that his abrupt leaving without a goodbye triggered Delores's memories of being a child alone in the house before school, because her parents had already left for work.

In actuality, David loved his wife very much, and didn't mean to hurt her. When it was his turn to speak, he told Delores that "when I leave in a hurry and just run out of the house, I am preoccupied by all the pressures and demands I have at work. It is not about you." Through dialoguing, he got in touch with why he got so irritated when she expressed her feelings on the "goodbye" issue—he felt that she was criticizing him. But the main thing he learned in the dialogue was that he *does* walk away and doesn't say goodbye, and that Delores makes incorrect assumptions about his behavior.

The dialogue is a powerful tool for understanding your partner's perspective, separate from yours. When it begins to make sense to you that your partner could perceive the issue in the way he/she does, you can sincerely say so. David was able to tell Delores, "It really makes sense to me that when I don't say goodbye in the morning, you feel as though I don't care." The key here is that when you say it, you mean it. That's validation.

Empathy. The final element of the Intentional Dialogue is empathy. Here, you share with your partner what you imagine he or she might be feeling. You put yourself in their place emotionally. You give your best guess, and then inquire, "Is that accurate?" Then you learn that their feelings may or may not be what you imagined them to be, and that they may be experiencing feelings you had no idea about. However, it *is* the way they feel. No one can argue about what someone else feels.

The empathy part of the dialogue helps both people become more sensitive to the feelings of the speaker. Empathy helps the speaker to discover: "What am I really feeling?" We are empowered when we name our feelings, rather than be awash in emotion. The empathy part of the dialogue is more interactive. The listener can help in this process. As the listener observes, tunes in, and witnesses the tears in the other's eyes or senses the anger in his/her body, it can help the listener tune in to a partner with a new level of depth and compassion. Sometimes the listener will suggest, based on noticing body language, a feeling that is accurate but the speaker has not yet named for him/herself. If the listener suggests feelings that are not accurate, it gives the speaker a chance to sort out what is true for them.

To review, the four steps of the Intentional Dialogue are: Mirroring, Summary, Validation, and Empathy. We recommend that you read *Getting the Love You Want* by Harville Hendrix and Helen LaKelly Hunt for a more in-depth presentation of the Intentional Dialogue.

Getting to Resolution through Dialogue

Recently we worked with a newly married couple that used the Intentional Dialogue to head off what would have been their typical fight. Instead they came to a good resolution. In their typical fight Ashley felt put down, bullied, and disrespected by her husband. Adam felt hurt by her reaction, since he believed that he was only trying to help.

The couple was meeting a friend, Marissa, that evening, and Adam wanted to bring up the issue of whether Marissa was planning to repay a loan they had jointly given her. Adam had brought up the topic with Ashley the evening before our session. According to Adam, Ashley immediately became defensive, saying, "Marissa told me her unemployment is running out and she has no money to get through the next few months." Adam took what she said to mean that his wife was going to back down and not ask about the loan. Even though Adam knew that Ashley was protective of the friend and sensitive to her situation, he experienced her defensiveness as a conversation stopper. He dropped it rather than arguing with her, and decided to wait until our next couples session the next day to talk about it again.

In their session with us, Ashley agreed to talk about the issue using the Intentional Dialogue. Because the dialogue is a structured way of communicating, it helps couples contain their emotional reactivity. In the dialogue, Ashley began as the speaker, and Adam was the listener. Ashley told Adam, "I first want you to know that I agree with you that the money needs to be repaid, and I also expect Marissa to repay it. I guess I did cut you off, but I was afraid that if we bring it up tonight when we have dinner with Marissa you'd be domineering, and 'lecture' her. She has so much she is dealing with now, I don't want to pressure her. I guess I don't trust you to handle things diplomatically."

Adam relaxed when he heard Ashley acknowledge that she did cut him off, and that she also wanted the loan repaid. When it was his turn to speak, he said, "I was so angry last night when I tried to bring up the subject and you cut me off; you just dismissed me. If we didn't have counseling today, I probably would have just shut up, gotten angry, and let you handle it with Marissa. I'd be imagining you'd be letting Marissa off the hook because you feel so sorry for her, and I'd be resentful. I probably would have exploded later and we would have had our usual fight." Adam welled up as he said softly, "I'm realizing that this was not about the money. What bothers me is how we treat each other."

As the listener, Ashley was able to acknowledge how much she'd hurt Adam when she cut him off. Both partners were grateful that they had the dialogue tool to create the safety to break an old, destructive pattern. Leaving our office holding hands and with a plan to talk with Marissa, they felt like a team, with each member playing an important role. They agreed that Ashley would bring up the topic at dinner, while Adam would listen and make some practical suggestions if that seemed appropriate. They found themselves actually looking forward to the conversation with their friend.

When to Dialogue

There are particular times in life when using the Intentional Dialogue tool can be an absolute relationship saver, such as the stress of caring for a sick relative or child, making a big purchase, a major rupture in your relationship like an affair, buying a home, serious illness, planning a vacation, a child going off to college, or retirement. The dialogue gives you an opportunity to deal directly with the issue together, rather than sweeping it under the rug and feeling alone with your concerns.

An approaching vacation can provide a good opportunity to practice dialogue skills. There are a lot of expectations regarding a vacation. Some people want to relax, while others may look forward to being with friends and family. Still others want to spend a lot of time alone. Some people want to tour on vacation, while others want to relax. Whatever the expectations are, it is important to be aware of them and to communicate them *before* you go away.

We'd like to share an example from our experience of how things can go awry when a couple fails to communicate before a vacation. Prior to a trip to Paris in the summer of 1991, we didn't talk about our expectations for the vacation. In many ways, it was an exciting time for us. Both of our children were in college and it was a time for us to start exploring other possibilities in our lives, one of which was a move from New York City to the Berkshires in Massachusetts.

But before moving, we decided to take a trip to Europe, something we had never done before as a couple. We were both very excited about this two-week vacation, which included visiting friends in Bavaria as well as visiting our daughter who was then a college student and working at Euro Disney in Paris that summer. We had carefully planned our itinerary for the whole trip. Unfortunately, we failed to talk beforehand about what truly mattered—our personal, individual expectations for the trip.

We arrived in Paris in the afternoon after a long overnight flight, during which we had not slept. When we got to the hotel, there was an enthusiastic note waiting for us from our daughter stating she would love to see us that evening at Euro Disney. Because we were so excited to see her, we left the hotel almost immediately, not having any idea how far away Euro Disney was from our hotel. Exhausted from our plane travel, we found ourselves on a very long ride on the Metro—many miles beyond the Paris city limits—to visit our daughter at her workplace.

Because we didn't talk about our expectations (indeed, we weren't even conscious of them), we were irritable with each other for the rest of the day and evening and didn't know why. Our mutual annoyance set the tone for the rest of our time in Paris. It wasn't until we got back home to the States that we became aware that we had failed to talk about something very important—our expectations for the trip.

For Bill, Paris is a city full of romance and excitement and he wanted to show Ani special places where he'd spent time in his youth. So on that first day, riding the subway straight out of Paris, he felt cheated. And because he wasn't aware of his expectations and needs, he felt disappointment, which he expressed as annoyance with Ani.

Ani, meanwhile, had one clear goal during their time in Paris, which was to see their eighteen-year-old daughter whom she had not seen since Christmas (she'd spent the second semester of her freshman year abroad). Ani had not thought much about what else she wanted to do in Paris. As a result, much of our time in Paris revolved around our daughter's work schedule. Ani felt Bill's irritation and reacted defensively, thinking that her need to spend time with her daughter should be equally important to him.

This trip had its high moments, no question. But it would have been more joyful if we had taken the time to talk about our expectations and needs beforehand, and created a plan to respect and accommodate each other's wishes. The lesson we learned is that it is important to talk about what you expect and want to do on your vacation, and to not hold back about your wishes and desires or try to please the other at your own expense. It will only backfire. Now, we always dialogue before a trip.

Practice for Compassionate Listening

MIRRORING AND SUMMARIZING

We suggest that you and your partner do a mirroring and summarizing exercise to share your expectations before important life events, such as a wedding, funeral, major vacation, and when either of you is upset about an issue, such as finances, parenting, sex, extended family, household chores. First, please review the instructions earlier in this chapter on mirroring. Then one of you suggests the topic, and asks the partner if he/she is willing to talk about it. Finally, agree on a time frame for the dialogue. A time frame is important: We find that couples can get into trouble when the dialogue goes on and on, and there is no agreed upon time frame.

One person begins talking about their expectations/concerns. Next, the other partner mirrors back what they heard, and summarizes. Then, switch so the other partner has a chance to speak about his/her expectations, while the first partner mirrors and summarizes. You can then start negotiating the differing needs you may have.

For example, if on vacation one partner wants

to spend a few hours being alone during the day and the other wants to spend a few hours walking along the beach and going swimming, talk about it first. It is very easy to assume that your partner knows what you need. You may not even know, yourself! Taking the time to talk beforehand will draw out from both of you what would most "light you up" on vacation.

Here is the bottom line: Whenever we are able to bridge the gap of communication and understanding, we move into a very intimate, connected place with our partner. We open up many more possibilities because we can draw on the creative resources of each other.

fourth heart tool:

MAKING ROOM FOR DIFFERENCES

Once the realization is accepted that even between the closest human beings infinite distances continue, a wonderful living side by side can grow, if they succeed in loving the distance between them which makes it possible for each to see the other whole against the sky.

—*Rainer Maria Rilke*

Friends of ours, Marie and Christie, told us about their different reactions to a movie they'd just seen. "I loved it!" said Marie afterward. She went on to say that it was one of the best movies she'd ever seen. Her partner, Christie, thought to herself that the movie had been awful. She also thought "no person in her right mind could like this movie." Silently, she became severely critical of Marie, thinking "she's moronic, idiotic, ridiculous," and then escalated into thinking, "Oh my God, I must be with the wrong person."

This is a version of catastrophic thinking. But fortunately, in this case, Christie had the presence of mind to ask Marie what she liked about the movie. Marie observed that she had loved the cinematography, the music, and the overall creativity of the production. Christie understood her partner's point of view, and was able to give up judging her character.

More than that, Christie began to see Marie as a separate person bringing an entirely different worldview to a shared experience. She actually began to find it quite interesting to be with someone who looked at things so differently, even though she had no need to change her own opinions about the movie. When Marie asked Christie what she thought of the movie, Christie was able to share her distaste for it without putting down Marie's conclusions. By becoming curious about each other's points of view, they felt close to each other in that moment, instead of arguing and judging. In short, we don't have to think like our partner to get along with them. We need to make room for differences, which include perceptions and feelings. This is our fourth heart tool.

Acknowledging differences can be particularly challenging for couples. Often partners, like Mark and Jana in the chapter on the first heart tool of Presence, get into power struggles because they don't know how to deal with their partner when he or she has a different point of view or is angry or upset with them. They feel threatened by differences. Wanting your partner to think and feel like you do is like asking them to be a clone of you. This gives you predictability and may lessen conflict, but it can lead to boredom and stifle your growth as an individual and as a couple. Diversity and variety contribute to intimacy and passion in your relationship.

Differentiation is a crucial step in a relationship. This has nothing to do with how independent a person is in his/her own right. A person can have his or her own career, friends, and interests, but still have a hard time saying, "This is me, different from you," in their intimate relationships. When we are differentiated we hold on to a separate sense of ourselves, with our own thoughts, feelings, opinions, and values even when others don't like it. We have a healthy sense of self, and we don't collapse, get defensive, or attack when others have a different point of view. We know we have a right to our ideas and feelings. Differentiation is a maturing process, entails developing self-awareness, and is a normal and healthy lifelong process.

In a new relationship, in an effort to move forward, we frequently put on blinders because we are so eager to experience greater intimacy and commitment. But the differences and qualities we don't like in our partners will come up eventually. Being able to differentiate is a developmental milestone in a relationship. If you let them, these differences can be great teachers, especially of tolerance and patience.

However, if you don't know how to deal with differences in a constructive way, it can be the beginning of the end of a relationship. Many partners get stuck in a power struggle. In some cases this struggle is vocal and argumentative, which may lead to one or both partners feeling too chronically angry to continue the relationship. In other cases, the struggle is passive, with one partner silently but reluctantly accommodating the other. This passive style has its own consequences: withdrawal and distancing. This can be the kind of marriage that ends suddenly and seemingly mysteriously, though in hindsight ex-partners may see many indications of issues that were never acknowledged or discussed.

We are not saying to accept all differences—by no means. There may be behaviors such as drinking, smoking, drug use, gambling, infidelity, physical or verbal abuse, unwillingness to work on problems in the relationship, or criminal behavior that is simply intolerable to you. These issues need to be discussed frankly and dealt with. It is important to be honest with yourself about what kinds of behaviors you can and cannot accept.

But in many cases, it's the little differences that get to us. How many times have you been driving in the car and your partner wants to make a detour? Couples frequently have conflicts about driving and end up in arguments. One partner wants to go straight and get to the destination as quickly as possible, while the other partner wants the flexibility to stop and explore. There is nothing wrong with either of these needs: one wants the certainty of knowing when he'll get to his destination, and the other wants variety and the freedom to go off the path.

In our relationship, Bill is the partner who wants to go straight from point A to point B, while Ani is the one who wants to meander when we travel. In the earlier years of our marriage, there was tension and sometimes arguments about the way we traveled in the car. Over the years, we've learned that if we are able to listen to what each of us wants, we can negotiate and make it a "win win." For example, if Bill wants to get to the beach by 3:00 p.m. and Ani wants to stop on the way for a late lunch, then we can decide ahead of time when we need to leave home. That way, both of us can get our needs met without forcing anything onto the other person, or making the other "wrong." The important thing is to think outside of the box and allow for differences between partners without clashing.

Of course, some differences involve issues more serious than driving. It is not uncommon that at mid-life, one partner begins to grow in personal development and the other doesn't. One partner becomes excited by new ways of understanding themselves and the world, and is beginning to question old roles and patterns and values. The other partner may feel satisfied with the way things are and not interested in growing or changing anything. A wedge can come between them when they can't talk and when they judge the other as wrong for changing or not changing.

Couples may be able to bridge these differences by being able to face them and talk together about what is going on. If differences can be accepted, the other partner may eventually open up to new ideas.

If your partner shows no interest in growing as a person, and growing is important to you and you are unable to talk about it in a productive way, you may want to get professional help as a couple to see if you can bridge your differences.

Practice for Making Room for Differences

To get started, you may want to try the following exercise, which you can do by yourself:

Lift your hands and let your palms face each other. Observe that one hand is slightly different from the other hand. Let the left hand represent your perception of reality and the right hand represent your partner's. Watch your palms exist close to each other, allowing room for both with space between them. Feel the energy of the connection.

What you can control is how you respond and how you treat each other when you negotiate differences. It's not a perfect world where you get everything you want. You do not have to have every one of your needs met to feel loved.

fifth heart tool:

COMMITMENT TO LOWER REACTIVITY

◇◇◇

Beyond our ideas of right-doing and wrong-doing,
there is a field. I'll meet you there.

—*Rumi*

In this chapter we give examples of practical ways couples can find their way out of stressful situations by together changing their attitudes and behavior in a creative way. They can cultivate "the field" Rumi talks about, and learn to respond, not react. The field refers to having a broader perspective. We have found that couples are quite innovative when their intention is to love each other, no matter how trying the circumstances may be. Commitment to lower reactivity is our fifth heart tool.

It is very difficult to change old, reactive patterns of attitude and behavior, which are hard-wired coping mechanisms from our past. These patterns of emotional reactivity show up as an over-reaction to a present situation by yelling, blaming, sarcasm, ridiculing your partner, name-calling, or threatening to leave. These behaviors trigger your partner to react in turn, and a downward cycle of reactivity can ensue. It is vital to stop this downward spiral before it gets abusive. It's okay to be angry, sad, or frustrated, but it is *never okay* to act out with violent behavior.

Avoidance is another form of reactivity. It is another way of coping with pain. When people don't know how to deal with conflict, they bottle it up and let resentments simmer. Avoidance leads to withdrawing affection, falling into hopelessness, and quitting. When this is the case, couples need a safe way such as the structure of Intentional Dialogue to break out of their avoidance.

What happens with emotional reactivity is that we are triggered by something in the present that brings up feelings from the past. We may not be conscious of what was triggered and all we are aware of now is that we feel unheard, shamed, criticized, unseen. In essence it is an overreaction.

It takes intentionality to change these old behavior patterns. It also takes attentiveness, ingenuity, and a sense of humor as well as a deep desire to get closer and be more intimate with your partner. When we have a lot of stress, we need strong heart tools to help us get out of those difficult moments. We hope you find them helpful and we encourage you to be creative in coming up with your own approaches.

Practices for Lowering Reactivity

CREATING CODE WORDS

Going to the couch. Cheryl and Scott had seen us for couples' therapy. They were a very nice and polite couple, who avoided topics that made them uncomfortable. Their avoidance created more distancing; they felt like roommates and the passion was draining from their relationship. They wanted to change these patterns, and found the mirroring technique in their sessions with us helped them to open up and feel safer talking about charged topics. They were able to practice this mirroring technique at home. Whenever they had a problem they would mirror back to each other, which helped them stay connected rather than defaulting into having a drink or sitting in front of the TV—the only options they'd previously had. They were able to develop a tool to deal with the stresses and tensions between them in a more effective way.

This couple eventually developed words to alert each other when they felt internal conflict. They used the words "going to the couch" as a verbal signal. This was a way of alerting the other to their distress in a loving way. Not only would they speak the words "going to the couch," but they would actually go to a couch in their house and begin to mirror the other person. The signal of "going to the couch" became a way of coming together in a loving and constructive way.

The first time they told us of their approach of "going to the couch" they expressed it with pride and excitement. They told us that for them to just think "I'm going to the couch" became a way of changing attitudes immediately, and it gave them hope and reassurance that they could safely discharge feelings. Just knowing that they were "going to the couch" and could trust they'd be listened to by their partner changed their way of thinking and feeling immediately.

Regaining control. We want to share an example of how an out-of-control couple found a tool to help them regain control. Patricia and Tim triggered in each other the physical and mental abuse they both received as children. It didn't take much provocation to initiate a physical altercation between them. In our earlier sessions we worked on lowering reactivity and physical violence. They made an agreement not to hit each other and they agreed to take time-outs when either one was volatile. As the sessions progressed and the couple was learning to slow down their reactivity and violence, they became aware in one of our sessions that they needed a strong reminder, a code word or phrase, to remind them not to react violently.

They came up with the code "red alert!" to warn the other partner that he/she was struggling and at the same time wanted to stay connected in a nonviolent way. Red alert! was a way for one partner to name his/her internal experience of feeling out of control, and was a way to warn the other. It helped them to know they had a mutually agreed-upon tool when they were in a heated situation. The red alert! signal was like a switch to turn down their reactivity in the moment. It gave Patricia and Tim a feeling of hope and confidence to know they could help each other stay in control when triggered. After they were more in control, they were able to begin to address their deeper issues.

CREATING YOUR OWN CODE WORD

As we have mentioned, there are various ways to change, and one of them is to change our words in a heated moment. That's what Patricia and Tim did when they came up with red alert!; they changed their words and that helped them contain their destructive behavior.

We'd like you to take a moment with your partner and think about what words you might use when you're very anxious, angry, or frustrated with each other. What will be your red alert?

More Practices: When Talking Doesn't Work

WHEN YOU GET TOO SERIOUS

We've been talking about different ways for couples to quickly get out of a negative spiral by changing their behavior. The next is a funny and entertaining approach we learned from our friends, Steve and Barbara. They both agree that when one finds the other bogged down in taking him/herself too seriously, the other will make a funny face to shift the energy. They will stick out a tongue or contort their face and then both usually start laughing. They both know this is a message to their partner to lighten up and not take things so seriously. It's perfect because it shifts from being intensely serious to being humorous. So instead of getting into an argument they get into a laughing mode in which they are playing and being silly with each other.

Making a face helps us laugh at ourselves and each other in a noncritical way. This is a big gift for couples who tend to be serious. This is a wonderful technique to do with your partner under stress *if* it's mutually agreed upon. The important thing is to let your partner know beforehand that it's a nonverbal way to lighten up, such as making a face, or being goofy or silly. Another benefit of being playful is that it loosens the tension around your heart and belly, which allows you to be more open-hearted— vital in an intimate relationship.

We would like you to think about a situation when humor helped you and your partner. If you are having a difficult moment with each other you might want to remember this funny and intimate moment when the two of you laughed. Humor touches us in a place of innocence and joy, and in every part of our being.

JUMPING IN THE LAKE

We want to give an example of lowering reactivity when talking is making it worse. A year after we met, we were on a camping trip in the White Mountains of New Hampshire. We were traveling around a beautiful lake and driving each other crazy. Both of us were so hurt, angry, and reactive, it was hard to take in the beauty around us. Talking was getting us nowhere; rather it was digging us into a pit of negativity and reactivity. Even though it was close to dusk, Ani said, "Let's jump in the lake," hoping it would break up our arguments. Bill kept thinking "I want to get away," but his better judgment knew that it was certainly better to jump in the lake than arguing in a car or being mad all night in a tent. So we parked the car, put on our bathing suits and walked toward the lake. We were both very angry at each other as we stepped into the water. But then a miraculous thing happened! As we proceeded to go into the cool water, our tensions started to drop away. And as our whole bodies immersed into the water we simultaneously started laughing and playing together.

Jumping in the water dissolved our negativity immediately, and we dropped our emotional stuff. In a split second, we went from being very angry and upset with each other, to feeling our love for each other. This was an incredibly quick change in our state of consciousness. Taking an action that is spontaneous, out of the ordinary, and mutually agreed upon, is a way to immediately change the energy between you. When both partners change their consciousness at the same time, it is a miraculous experience. The next time you and your partner are having a difficult moment, and talking is making it worse, and all you are doing is blaming each other, see if you can be creative and come up with your own version of jumping in the lake. It may be taking a walk, going for a run or hike, putting on music and dancing, or it may be going swimming if that is a viable option. Whatever your version of changing your behavior with your partner is, it can be a tremendous gift to your relationship. "Jumping in the lake" has become a mutual code word between us.

WALKING AND TALKING

Many couples take a walk to lessen tension, frustration, and anger between themselves and their partner. This sounds like a very simple technique, which it is, and it works. One couple told us that taking walks and talking is saving their marriage after an affair.

This can be done in a few minutes or can be a long hike involving several hours. The walking can be in the neighborhood, in a park, or in a more secluded natural setting in the woods. The important thing is that it helps both partners shift their consciousness from frustration to a more neutral state of being. One couple used this technique when they hiked and walked side by side. This was especially meaningful to the woman, because in the past her husband had usually charged ahead of her, and she constantly felt she had to scramble to catch up, or be alone at her own pace. Saying the words, "taking a walk" in this case, is like using the code word "peace" while under stress with your partner.

FROM BOREDOM TO DANCING IN THE DARK

Katie and Leslie told us they accidentally discovered a way to break up their monotonous daily routine which could get boring. They found that sometimes when they were bored they found themselves starting to argue with each other about small things, almost as a way to connect after not being with each other all day. One winter night they were listening to music on a radio station that was several hundred miles away in Toronto, Canada. It was an oldies station and the only way they could listen to it with no interference was to turn out the lights. Since they live in the country, far from street lights, it gets very dark when the lights are out. They discovered that complete darkness created an unexpected magic and romance. To their delight, they found themselves dancing in the dark. Now they have a new ritual. At least once a week, especially on cold winter nights, they turn off the lights. They also find that sitting in the pitch dark is a form of meditation that quiets the mind, and gets them ready to go to bed that evening. They use this approach to slow down after a day of work and to be present with each other. Sometimes they sit in silence on the couch together, sometimes they talk to each other, and sometimes they dance. But the most important thing is to be with each other in a quiet place. We've tried their approach and find it peaceful and soothing to the mind. We use our minds all day long and it's nice to have the transition of slowing down before going to bed.

The examples we've given in this chapter all involve lowering reactivity while *with* your partner. Sometimes, this is not possible, and one partner needs "a time out," to de-stress alone. They may need to retreat to a quiet place in the home or the woods to meditate, read, work-out, practice yoga, or use one of the tools we mentioned earlier in the chapter on Presence, such as the Three Breath Technique or the heart-focused meditation. When one of you needs to be alone to calm down, it is important to keep the connection with your partner by respectfully informing them that you need space. But assure them that you will be back to address whatever issues have not been discussed after you have calmed down.

Many of us have been taught to believe we have no choice but to stay stuck when we are angry, frustrated, upset, or bored. However we're always able to change and make a different decision under any situation. We do not have to stay stuck in our old way of reacting under stress. As a matter of fact when we make a decision to change from reactivity to neutrality to love, we have transformed that experience, and we have transformed ourselves and each other.

sixth heart tool:

TRANSFORMING HURT AND RESENTMENT INTO FORGIVENESS

◇◇

If you were going to die soon and had only one phone call you could make, who would you call and what would you say? And why are you waiting?

—*Stephen Levine*

To keep love alive, we need ways to heal the hurt and resentment that comes up in all relationships. When one partner is hurt or resentful, usually the other partner is, too. Dealing courageously with these emotions offers opportunities to grow and mature in a relationship. Transforming hurt and resentment into forgiveness is our sixth heart tool.

Clinging to Pain

It is easy to hold on to old hurts and resentments, letting them fester over time. It is easy to rationalize why you have to protect your heart by staying closed off from your partner. The problem with this approach is that nothing gets resolved. There are many reasons why people hold on to hurt. One is that it is hard to endure the pain of emotional wounds and focusing on the cruel and unfathomable acts of our partner convinces us that we are justified in our distress.

Another reason we may hold on to the pain is because we think that it will protect us from more suffering. "If I stay closed, nothing like this can ever happen to me again," we tell ourselves. Still another major reason we cling to hurt is because we don't have tools to deal with difficult emotions. It takes maturity, and sometimes professional help, to make sense of our hurt and let it go.

There are different ways people express hurt: anger, being quiet, physically distancing, or being sullen, withdrawn, and depressed. We might get sarcastic. Or we could take it up a notch through name-calling, threatening to leave, ridiculing our loved one. It can escalate to yelling, hitting, pushing, and threatening to harm your partner. Other, more passive, but nonetheless hostile and damaging behavior is turning your back on your partner, walking out, threatening to leave, excessive criticism, sarcasm, chronic defensiveness, and giving them the "silent treatment." These behaviors deeply hurt our partners.

When a person is abusive it is almost always related to that person's deeper feelings of hurt, loneliness, despair, and hopelessness. These feelings require serious and sustained professional care.

Exit Strategies

In Imago Therapy, we use the word "exits" to describe ineffective coping behaviors to deal with hurt and fear of intimacy in relationships. Exits are ways that we emotionally or behaviorally leave the relationship. Some exits take the form of addictions, including alcoholism and other substance abuse, gambling, pornography, workaholism, and internet addiction. Other exits take the form of affairs, threats to leave, and violence. All of these behaviors are ways to avoid dealing with hurt feelings or fears, but they are the equivalent to having one foot out of the door. Exits leave emotional scars on your partner, resolve nothing, and are not easy to remedy.

By acting out through exits, you are not dealing with what is really bothering you or giving yourself a chance to resolve these issues with your partner. It is like hanging off a cliff, creating a lot of drama but accomplishing nothing useful. Keep in mind that when you act out, you are using only the primitive, impulsive part of your brain. You're leaving your rational brain out of the decision-making process. You're also not coming from your heart.

Many issues can be resolved, but it takes plenty of work, dedication, and the willingness to share your own fears, vulnerabilities, insecurities, and fear of intimacy with your partner. The next time you feel like acting out, don't do it! Remember that you have more brain power available. Bring the focus back to yourself: Ask "how am *I* hurting, and how can I soothe myself right now?" Take some time to think about the consequences of your actions.

Much negative behavior is subtle, and we are not aware of it until we get feedback from others. Becoming aware of one's negativity is a humbling process. But over time, as we accept that we are imperfect beings who hurt others even if not intentionally, we can become aware when we are veering into negative territory. This is an ongoing process of both letting go of harsh self-judgment and, at the same time, taking responsibility for how we affect others. This is why we need our partners to tell us when we have wittingly or unwittingly hurt them. It is an opportunity to grow.

An example is Jenny, who is a big giver in her family. In one of our sessions, after her husband David had declined her request to clean out the shed because he was maxed out with projects, she said under her breath, "You're just lazy." David not only heard what she said but also picked up the bitter edge in her voice.

Fortunately, he was able to tell her in a non-reactive and non-blaming way that she had hurt his feelings. Jenny had not been consciously aware of her tone of voice and hostility until David told her how her words had landed on him. Once she became aware of this, she started to become aware of her subtle negativity. Gradually, Jenny was able to take responsibility for her behavior, accept that it was okay to ask for help, and take care of herself better by calmly communicating to her husband that she needed more consistent, ongoing help from him. And he was able to hear her when she spoke from a calm and non-accusatory place.

In addition to stating your feelings and positions

calmly, you can shift the energy in your relationship by sharing appreciations and positive things with your partner each day, as we suggested in the chapter on the second heart tool of Appreciations. This is quite an assignment when you are stuck in hurt and resentment, and yet it is an important way to shift out of resentment into a more positive state of being. Each appreciation, no matter how small, will have a strengthening effect on your relationship. We see this as "preventive medicine."

The Work of Forgiveness

It is easy to be absorbed by our own hurt and to feel justified in our reactions. However, as we noted earlier, if you're hurt, the chances are good that your partner is hurt, too. To begin any forgiveness process, it is important to understand that your partner is also suffering in some way. To be able to look outside of yourself and objectively see another person's perspective goes a long way towards forgiveness.

This can be particularly challenging when there has been an affair, which requires an enormous amount of time, work, and commitment from both partners in order to heal. We are thinking of a couple we worked with several years ago. Megan had discovered Carl's affair from cell phone bills. Carl initially lied and dismissed her accusations. Eventually, he owned up to the truth—he'd been having an affair for the past six months. Megan was devastated. But because she and Carl had young children and loved each other, she decided to give him another chance. He realized he didn't want to lose his wife. They were motivated to stay together and learn what had gone wrong in their marriage.

Importantly, each of them was willing to look at his/her own part in the decline of their relationship. It helped Megan that Carl owned up to his behavior, and was able to listen to her pain. He also was willing to put her first, and made a commitment to completely end the affair and to work on the marriage. This commitment—and action to back it up—helped to re-create trust.

Eventually, Carl began to talk about his wife's distancing and withdrawal, which he realized did not justify the affair but had contributed to the problems in the marriage. He'd never before brought up his dissatisfactions with Megan directly, and this was a big step for him. Because he had taken responsibility for hurting her, Megan was able to hear her husband's pain. She was able to see she had withdrawn from him well before the affair.

When each partner felt that the other was willing to understand their deep hurt, they were able to move forward and take steps to create more connection with each other. Carl was able to hear Megan's feelings of betrayal that he'd had an affair, her outrage that he'd blatantly lied to her about it, and that he was a workaholic who rarely made himself available to her or the children. She heard his pain about feeling emotionally neglected by her, as she over-focused on the children, took him for granted, nagged him, and withdrew sexually.

Carl was struggling with deep guilt. What ultimately helped him to forgive himself was to decide to be fully present to Megan and her hurt feelings. He extended himself to her by asking her how he could be of help. She told him "I want you to take the time to listen to me, and put me first." Over time, he demonstrated to her that he could listen to her deep hurt about his affair and he practiced the heart tool of Presence. The more they were able to understand and communicate their feelings and needs and make their relationship a priority by spending quality time together, the more they were able to forgive. Slowly and with great effort, they began to create a new relationship, based on honesty and loving connection. They were proud of their ability to change old patterns and give themselves a deeper and more fulfilling relationship.

The healing process starts by accepting that you are indeed hurt. An effective way to deal with our pain is to ask our partner to listen to us so that we can share our feelings in the safe "container" of a structured dialogue. This is usually not a one-shot deal—you may need many dialogues. It can help greatly when we feel that our partner listens, understands, and validates our thoughts and feelings.

Mark Nepo writes in *The Book of Awakening*, "It is useful to realize that the word *forgive* originally meant both to give and receive—to 'give for' ... It is hard to comprehend how this works, yet the mystery of true forgiveness waits in letting go of our ledgers of injustice and retribution in order to regain the feeling in our heart." When we truly forgive another, we free our hearts. It takes maturity and compassion and work to forgive and let go. The hurt individual may need to move through a grieving process as Elizabeth Kubler Ross describes it: moving from denial, to acknowledging strong emotions of betrayal, anger, sadness, and depression to eventually being able to let go.

Whenever couples are able to work through differences and old hurts, and to move forward by prioritizing their relationship and feeding it, they are transforming hurt into forgiveness. When any of us is deeply hurt, what we most crave is the compassionate presence of our loved one. By focusing on love and connection as you address deep hurts, you can move toward healing and forgiveness.

Practice for Letting Go of Hurt and Resentment

This practice is meant to help you release the hurt and resentment in your heart. It is not to excuse anyone for how they have hurt you with their words or actions.

Sit in a quiet place where you will have privacy. Start by taking slow deep breaths to create a feeling of safety and connection with your self. Become deeply present to yourself.

Close your eyes and think of someone, possibly your partner, towards whom you are holding resentment.

Reflect on whether you want to let go of this resentment. This may involve taking into account the cost of holding on to the resentment. Is it causing agitation, anger, depression? When we hold on to resentment towards someone, we have a strong negative connection with that person.

You may or may not want to restore a positive connection, but you may want to be free of the negativity. You may want to go into a neutral state in regards to this person.

The next step is to decide "Do I want to let go of this negative connection?"

If you decide you want to let go, start the healing process by taking a few moments to think of 3 things you appreciate about this person, despite your hurt.

Next, acknowledge your hurt feelings about the situation, such as sadness, hurt, disappointment, betrayal, anger, or feeling misunderstood. Feel your feelings without having to do anything about them.

Accept the reality that the hurtful action happened, and there is nothing you can do now to change that.

Reflecting on what happened, think about how the other person may have perceived the situation, and how they may have been feeling about it at the time. They might have also been feeling disappointed, hurt, and misunderstood. You might want to imagine them as a hurt child. Challenge yourself to put yourself in the other person's shoes. This is the beginning of empathy and compassion.

Sit a little longer. Let the chest wall soften, and breathe into your heart. If you are not letting go, be patient and compassionate with yourself. This practice often needs to be repeated several times. Just starting is a big step.

–adapted from Marci Shimoff's "forgiveness practice"

seventh heart tool:

NURTURING PASSION

◇◇

Sexual energy is the primal and creative energy of the universe. All things that are alive come from sexual energy … In humans, sexual energy can be creative at all levels—physical, emotional, and spiritual. In any situation—where we feel attraction, arousal, awakening, alertness, passion, interest, inspiration, excitement, creativity, enthusiasm—in each of these situations, sexual energy is at work.

—*Deepak Chopra*

On our honeymoon, we learned something profound about keeping passion and love alive. While at a resort in Mexico, we took a walk one evening through the small village next to the resort. It was just before sunset. As we walked by one small house—a shack by our standards—the front door was open and we saw the sparsely furnished room inside. There were hammocks for beds, and a single, bare lightbulb hanging from the ceiling. But what really caught our attention, and our hearts, was the scene unfolding outside the house.

There, on a picnic table, was a transistor radio playing dance music. Enchanted, we watched as a young couple danced enthusiastically to the lively music. They were smiling and murmuring to each other. We thought of all the couples in the States who at that very moment were probably at home spending their evening catching up on work from the office, or sitting in front of a computer screen or TV. And here was this couple, enjoying one of the few material things they had, and having a blast! We thank them for reminding us that it truly is the simple things in life, and the intention to connect, that create passion.

Most of us see passion as sexual passion, but it can also be the excitement of spending enjoyable time together, as we saw with the couple in Mexico. Both are forms of passion and intimacy. Nurturing Passion is our seventh heart tool.

It can be devastating when one partner loses passion in a relationship. Passion can fade for several reasons: tension, anger, major arguments, or a breach of trust such as an affair. These usually undermine a couple's ability to be emotionally and physically close with each other. Also, passion can fade because it's not cultivated but put on the back burner while other needs and responsibilities such as earning an income, parenting children, or caring for an ill relative take precedence. Over time, sexual energy may shift for one or both partners. There is less sexual excitement, which is often the result of stress or bodily changes such as lower hormone levels. Many people experience a loss of libido with age, but that still doesn't mean there's a loss of interest in sex. When sexual desire is diminished because of circumstances, it doesn't mean it can't return, but it will require time and focus to reignite the passion.

Passion can also fade because of familiarity of spending years together. The neurotransmitters involved in sexual passion are dopamine, norepinephrine, and oxytocin. According to Norman Doidge, MD, dopamine and aspects of norepinephrine are also involved with novelty. "Sometimes when you hear people complaining about monogamy as being boring it's not that their mate is boring, it's just that there's a certain amount of routine involved in monogamous relationships or long-term, steady relationships ...You should pay some attention to the fact that if you want to maintain a long-term relationship, you're going to have to do certain things to inject some novelty into it" (from "How Love Rewires the Brain [and Other Romantic Secrets of Brain Chemistry]" an on-line discussion hosted by the National Institute for the Clinical Application of Behavioral Medicine). As we discuss later in this chapter creating the unexpected and novelty into your relationship will go a long way towards keeping passion alive. So if passion has faded in your relationship, we want to offer some suggestions. At the end of this chapter you will find some practices to restore passion.

If one or both of you has been hurt, trust needs to be restored, and that requires talking about the hurt. This process may take days, weeks, or even longer when there has been a severe breach of trust, or emotional or physical abuse. Healing from an affair can take months or years. Sometimes, one partner will not see that they have been hurtful, but the other partner is extremely hurt and may feel abused. It is only by talking this out and understanding each other's perspectives that a shift back to stability is possible. Practicing Presence, Appreciation, and Listening (PAL), and the other tools offered in this book will contribute to restoring passion.

We have found that there may be less sexual desire and activity with couples who don't deal with issues that come up between them. These couples need help to talk about issues they may be avoiding so that these unstated worries or concerns don't show up through avoiding physical connection.

We worked with one couple, Ted and Caroline, who finally were able to confront directly an issue they'd never talked about. Ted was 100 pounds overweight. Neither of them brought up this topic in sessions: both were in denial, and their sexual relationship was all but dead. After some time, Caroline found the courage to tell Ted that she loved him, but that she was losing her desire to be sexual with him because of his weight. Caroline had been reluctant to tell him this because she didn't want to hurt his feelings. Also, she tended to avoid speaking up on important issues because her father had never listened to her—an old but powerful story in her life.

When she finally mustered the courage to bring up his weight problem, Ted blew up with the anger Caroline had expected. But with our help, he was able to calm down and hear Caroline say, "I love you, and I'm not going anywhere, but it's hard for me to be sexually aroused when you're so overweight."

Eventually he was able to give up his old story that he was simply being rejected by a woman, and he was able to take in that Caroline loved him and wanted to be close to him sexually. He was motivated to take charge because he didn't want to lose his sexual relationship with her, and more importantly he didn't want to lose her love. Ted found a program to help him lose weight. Even though he's still working on weight loss and making lifestyle changes, the couple's ability to talk about this sensitive subject helped both partners to become passionate again. By being honest, Caroline broke through her old story that a man would never listen to her, or that she could never get her needs met by a man.

When stability and connection have been restored in a relationship, many couples feel closer emotionally and, in turn, will feel more loving and passionate towards each other. This may result in more sexual activity. What follows are more ideas for restoring passion.

Enhancing Body Image

An important prerequisite for passion is becoming aware of how we think and feel about ourselves and our bodies. If we see ourselves as beautiful, loving, sensual individuals, then we will create that reality in our relationships with our loved ones. If we see ourselves as ineffective, inadequate, or unattractive, we will bring that perception into our relationships, and that may stifle our sexual desire.

To a large degree, becoming more sensual is an inside job. The way to work on it is to become aware of how you talk to yourself about your body, and learn to be more accepting and positive about yourself. Our culture is image-driven with little range in what is considered attractive. We don't have to buy into these culturally defined images. We've seen couples of all shapes, ages, and appearances who are vital and alive sensually and sexually.

The Play of Love

To restore passion to your relationship, don't overlook the direct approach. Have a conversation about what each of you wants sexually and what turns you on, so that your partner knows what gives you pleasure. You can't expect your partner to turn you on if you've shut down and don't communicate what pleases you. Talking openly about your expectations about what each of you would like from the other is a very basic way to make sure you're on the same erotic page with your partner.

The more you can be aware of what excites you, the more you can communicate this to your partner and be able to create mutual sexual satisfaction. Make passion a joy, not a task. Let yourselves have fun. You don't have to be perfect. You can be awkward. All you need to do is show the willingness to play with sexual energy, a potent element of our life force. Sex is not a job; it is the play of love. Don't get caught up in performance.

And don't give up on passion! Intimacy and passion go together. Remember, passion is mental which means we can change our mindset, and we can do this at any age. We have known couples who face severe physical challenges, such as paraplegia, who keep the channel of sensuality and sexuality open between them.

Practices for Nurturing Passion

GUIDED IMAGERY: NURTURING PASSION

First read the entire practice, and then put down the book and let yourself experience the imagery. You can also record the imagery, and play it back.

Find a quiet spot, close your eyes and think about your partner at a time when there was great passion between you. Remember the circumstances, the setting, and what you were doing to or for each other. Allow yourself to fully be in this passionate experience. Now, tune into the arousal you're feeling in your body. Be aware of where in your body you are aroused; just be conscious of that as you think about that pleasurable experience.

CREATING A RITUAL FOR PASSION

Some couples who keep sexual passion alive over many years make it part of their regular routine. One couple, Janice and Chuck, who have grown children living out of the home, look forward to Saturday mornings in bed, which is their special time to give pleasure to each other. This couple had dealt with discord at times in their marriage, but throughout it all they usually made time for their Saturday mornings in bed, which was a strong glue for them.

TALKING IT THROUGH

It may be helpful to talk with your partner about some of your stresses and frustrations with loss of sexuality in a nonjudgmental way. The block to being sexual is often an emotional one. By talking about our feelings and fears we can alleviate some, if not all, of the emotional blockage, which will help us feel closer.

The other thing to remember is that the desire or need for sexual activity differs between couples, just as it does between individuals. Although research shows that couples with a good sexual relationship tend to be happier, for some couples a strong sexual connection is simply less important. They still can be loving, devoted, and intimate.

If one partner would like more sex, it is important that this partner voice his/her needs in a positive and non-blaming way. To desire your partner is, after all, a good thing! We suggest that the partner who feels less desire listen openly. This doesn't mean engaging in sex because you feel obligated to, or in any way compromising yourself. It means to be understanding of your partner's needs and making the effort to be sensual and sexual. The pleasure of enjoyable sexual experiences feeds the desire for more.

FROM ROUTINE TO VARIETY AND EXCITEMENT

With all of the time commitments and stresses crowding the lives of modern couples, it is critical to spend regular time together free of distractions. To enliven and enrich the relationship, taking ourselves out of the normal routine of our lives can be vital.

This is where creating novelty comes into play.

One couple we know is taking advantage of the fact that their daughter is in summer day camp by taking one day off a week from work to be together. One hot afternoon, they took a nap and spontaneously found themselves engaged in passionate lovemaking.

We enjoy surprise dates. Once when it was Ani's turn to plan something, she blindfolded Bill and took him on a car ride, looping around the neighborhood so that he wouldn't figure out where they were. Then she drove up their lawn, not the driveway, and escorted him, still blind-folded, into their den where she'd created a passion nest with pillows, aroma therapy oils, flowers, and romantic music. Imagination has no bounds.

Getting away as a couple from your home environment on a regular basis is important. And it does not require a lot of money; rather use your imagination to plan a fun time, away from your usual routine. You might find a bed and breakfast in a neighboring community or nearby city. You could pitch a tent in a nearby campground or house swap with friends or relatives or housesit for someone who is on vacation.

We suggest that all couples who want to renew and strengthen their relationship get away as frequently as once a month, or at the least every six weeks. Even twenty-four hours away can make a big difference. It requires some attention to schedule time away with your partner on a regular basis, but it is vital to put this kind of energy into your relationship. It doesn't matter where you go for a weekend adventure, as long as you have the intention to be with your partner during this period of time. If you schedule one or two days away with your partner, be clear about your intention that this time period is for the two of you.

Recently, we went on our monthly getaway to one of our favorite places, a rustic retreat center in central Massachusetts. We were very clear that our intention was to be with each other as well as for each of us to have some alone time. There was no electricity at this place, so we would not be distracted by telephones, computers, or other electronics. This made it quite clear that we were going to have some time playing and being romantic with each other, along with some time individually to reflect. We gave ourselves twenty-four hours of enjoying each other without the usual distractions of everyday life. Time alone together is a nutrient that feeds our relationship, encouraging it to stay healthy and continue to bloom.

Another time, we went to the same retreat center and used part of an afternoon for each of us to create vision boards of what we wanted in our relationship. We brought a shoebox with images and words we'd already cut out from a variety of magazines and some poster board and glue, and we truly had fun with it, sharing what we'd each done and talking about how we might move closer to our respective relationship visions.

To keep a relationship young and vibrant, you need to create variety and activity. It doesn't happen by lounging around watching TV, tweeting on your phone, or sitting in front of a computer in separate rooms. One of the things we do is head out to the Paradise Inn, a motel in rural Vermont. It's a place we found over ten years ago and return to at least once a year. One of the great things about this place is that some of the rooms come equipped with a whirlpool and a sauna. Nearby is a ski area, and a great Mexican restaurant. Talk about a stress-reducing vacation! Just thinking about going to the Paradise Inn puts us in a romantic state of mind. The combination of good exercise and good food puts us in a loving, sexual mood. We combine the pleasures of the outdoors with the pleasures of the indoors.

GUIDED IMAGERY:
DISCOVERING YOUR OWN PARADISE

First read the entire practice, and then put down the book and let yourself experience the imagery. You can also record the imagery, and play it back.

We'd like you to think about your own Paradise Inn. Where do you go with your partner to get away and have a romantic, relaxing, and playful time? Take a moment to think about where you go to enjoy your "paradise." If you don't have one at the present time, think about where you went to experience paradise earlier in your relationship. It may have been camping, going to the beach, or taking a ride in the country. Think about how it felt to go to your special place, and the particular kind of pleasure you experienced there with your partner.

When you have a place in mind, write it down, and then think about what you'd like to do with your partner on this trip. The next step is to ask your partner to go away with you. Tell him/her how important it is to get away so that the two of you can feel closer. If your partner would prefer to do something else, negotiate. You may be able to fulfill both wishes, or alternate. Or you may discover an alternative.

Intention is important! The reason to get away is to become closer and more loving with each other. When you tell your partner that you want to spend this time to be loving, it will be hard for him/her to refuse. We need to put aside time to love our partners, just as we put aside time for work, family, hobbies, and other responsibilities. Remember, when you first got together with your partner, you moved mountains to see each other. If you don't feel love with your partner, other aspects of your life are diminished too. It's like sitting for a long time in a room without windows.

Regularly feeding your relationship is essential to its life force. Taking just one day a month to get away will work wonders to reawaken passion, excitement, and intimacy between you.

eighth heart tool:

SEEING YOUR PARTNER
AS YOUR TEACHER

Each person who enters our life, every experience we have, is a teacher. Some things we learn amaze us, some trouble us. Everyone we have loved has become a part of us... And no relationship created in Love can ever die.

—*John E. Welshons*

Any time we learn from another person, that person becomes our teacher. We have many teachers in our life, but our most influential teacher can be our partner. We are challenged to be our authentic self and to be connected with them in the deepest, most intimate way. We are challenged to grow emotionally and spiritually. There is great beauty in recognizing our partner as our teacher. Acknowledging your partner as your teacher is the eighth heart tool. The purpose of this chapter is to give you tools to maximize the teacher potential of your relationship.

In a conscious relationship where each partner embraces learning from the other, the individuals flourish as love and trust grow. They walk side by side as equal, empowered partners. Their loving connection has the power to foster goodness and care to the larger world.

Our partner gives us a fresh way to experience the world. As we discussed in an earlier chapter, if our partner were exactly like us, we'd be terribly bored. Our challenge is to work with the differences in a way that produces growth. The way our partner thinks about the world, feels about the world, and behaves may be quite the opposite of our own thoughts, feelings, and behaviors. It is in those differences that treasures lie, just waiting to be discovered. This is the place where we can discover disowned or undeveloped parts of ourselves, and consciously evolve them. In addition to developing more of our untapped potential, when we are teachers to each other, we give ourselves the possibility of generating creative solutions to gnarly problems that in the past might have kept us stuck in reactivity or rigidity.

Most couples have vastly different styles in reactivity. Usually one partner is the "charger" and one dampens his or her charge and reacts with more withdrawal. In Imago terminology, one is the "lightning bolt" and one is the "turtle." These basic patterns are responses to stress and get hard-wired in the "old" part of our brains. By enlisting our partner as our teacher, we learn to lower the old fight-flight-freeze patterns and instead invite the more evolved part of our brain, the pre-frontal cortex, to help us evolve new patterns. By being open to our partner as teacher, we can help each other learn new ways to handle conflict and uncomfortable situations.

In our relationship, this primarily came up in regard to parenting, with Ani, the under-reactor, taking a more permissive approach to her kids, and Bill, the charger, as stepdad, wanted more accountability. When conflict came up, Bill would want to quickly confront the situation. Ani thought that her choice to under-react and ignore was the better way to respond because she thought it prevented a confrontation and preserved connection (of course it did neither). Our opposite styles would lead to tension and conflict between us, and we'd argue about who had the right approach. As we matured and became open to seeing the other as a teacher, the hard lines between us grew softer, and we could begin to hear beyond who had the "right" or "wrong" approach. Because we respected each other, and believed the other had our best interests at heart, we could calm down and listen to each other. Bill learned it was good to be more patient. Ani learned from Bill that sometimes you need to confront. By talking about it, we opened up ways to deal with situations each of us could accept. In hindsight, this sounds easy. Actually it represented a lot of relationship work: staying permeable to learning from each other meant that we had to shift some deeply ingrained habitual patterns that we were attached to and even shift a sense of our identity as individuals.

We want to share a few more examples from our experience of the potential learning we can have when we embrace each other as a teacher.

Ani: Learning from Bill

When Bill and I met, I was terrible about punctuality. I multitasked constantly and was proud of it. Inevitably, I underestimated how much time something would take and I was often late, though I didn't expect others to be on time either. If I was kept waiting, I'd always find something to do, or even feel relieved that they were late because I was usually running behind.

This did not work for Bill. He hated waiting for me and felt I was being inconsiderate. That did not fit with my self-image of being a considerate person, and I would often respond dismissively by saying something like, "What's the big deal? It's only a few minutes." But the truth was, it really *did* bother me that my behavior was upsetting the man I loved. I felt tense and pressured every time we had to go somewhere. I finally took responsibility for my behavior and recognized that this was an area where I had something to learn. I began to ask Bill to help me to estimate the time I'd need to get ready and the time it would take to drive to our destination.

Bill has been a wonderful teacher for me with regard to punctuality. He must have inherited the genes of his paternal grandfather, who was a trainman. He still has his grandfather's big, gold trainman's pocket watch! By now, I have integrated time awareness into my life and no longer need to rely on Bill's help. I'm nearly always on time—or even early—and I'm a lot less stressed!

Bill's contribution to my education in time awareness has benefited my workshop planning as well. I am usually excited by the many creative ideas and experiences I want to include in a workshop. Bill helps by listening to me, and helping me prioritize what I want to accomplish. Finally, we arrive at a realistic estimate of how much time each segment will take. I end up keeping things simpler and more elegant. Most of all, I'm relaxed and feel that what I'm giving is enough.

Bill has also taught me the value of routine. Every morning, he sits in meditation for twenty minutes. This regularity adds rhythm and comfort to my day, whether I join him or not. He has also helped me experience the value of celebrations. For the most part, my family was modest in its celebrations. We did birthdays, Thanksgiving, Hanukkah, and Passover very simply. By contrast, Bill comes from a large family that throws grand, festive celebrations for Thanksgiving and Christmas.

I remember when I first met Bill's family at a Christmas gathering at his sister's home. The house was elaborately decorated, and the table was set magnificently. I couldn't believe all the food! The atmosphere was warm, welcoming, and inclusive. There were gifts for my children and me, even though we were brand new to the family.

Bill also shows me that we can celebrate everyday life with small, loving acts. He brings me flowers and balloons, and writes me creative, affectionate notes. On many winter mornings, I look out the window to see "I love you" written in the snow. He has inspired me to give more, and to give more in a creative way. His knowledge of birding and love of the natural world has enriched my life tremendously. He also has the biggest heart of any man I've ever met. He's taught me to welcome all of my emotions. This has been tremendously freeing. And he's a master of play and magic, and creating silly, playful moments spontaneously. I cherish that he's taught me to be much more light-hearted.

Bill: Learning from Ani

When I first became a therapist, I worked primarily with individuals. Ani inspired me to expand my practice to include groups, workshops, and couples. Left to my own devices, I'd still be working with clients one-on-one. She inspired me to stretch and thereby give to more people at one time.

Before we met, Ani was a networker. She inspired me to work with her to create a holistic network of professionals. I loved the camaraderie and socializing of the networking groups. They inspired me to create new ways of working with people, and that led me to work with men's issues, leading men's groups, and creating a workshop called Making Peace with Your Father.

Looking back, Ani's difficulty with time management also taught me a great deal. I learned that I could step back, refrain from judging, and welcome differences in the way we each got ready to go out into the world. This rethinking process developed into the NOW principle (Not to judge; stay Open; Welcome differences) that we teach in our workshops.

Ani also introduced me to yoga and meditation. These practices opened me up to a spiritual side of myself that I had put away a long time ago. Through yoga and meditation, I continue to learn that we are all interconnected.

Finally, Ani gave me the opportunity to be a stepfather, which opened my world to loving two precious human beings, Allison and Derek. My stepchildren have also been wonderful teachers to me. I have learned to be more patient, more giving, and deal better with anger.

Practices for Seeing Your Partner (and Others) as Your Teacher

DISCOVER WHAT YOU'VE LEARNED FROM YOUR PARTNER

Take a few moments to think about the positive characteristics of your partner. Write down these attributes and put a check next to those that you have adopted from him or her. Next, reflect on the aspects of your partner that you've had the most difficulty with, and how you have grown because of them. You may be surprised by the influence your partner has had on your life. Share your reflections with your partner.

DISCOVER WHAT YOU LEARNED FROM YOUR PARENTS OR CAREGIVERS

Our first role model for relationship is our parents' relationship. We want you to be aware of both the positive and negative relationship traits you learned. Why? Because what we experience as children deeply imprints itself and, unless brought to awareness, we will unconsciously live out the patterns (both good and bad) that were modeled. Many people, and you may be among them, saw your parents' unhappiness and decided long ago not to be like them; you are dismayed to see their patterns repeat in your relationships. The first thing is not to judge yourself as doing anything wrong. Unless we consciously change patterns, they will repeat. At the same time, we also want to appreciate the positive behaviors, values, and attitudes we learned growing up and to strengthen them.

To become aware, it is helpful to write down the traits, both positive and negative, you saw in your parents' relationship/s, and write down the ones you see in yourself. We suggest you share this with your partner.

DISCOVER WHAT YOU LEARNED FROM OTHER COUPLES

Couples need role models of healthy, loving relationships, especially as they move from the early honeymoon stage to a more committed relationship in which they must identify shared values and create a relationship vision. Our role models help us to identify what is important to us, motivate us to grow, and help us to see how we can contribute our love to the larger world.

Reflect for a moment on couples you know who are in a loving, committed relationship. As you think of these couples and their values, notice what you admire, notice how they treat each other and express themselves, notice how they enjoy each other and whether they are happy in each other's presence. Are you expressing the qualities you admire in them in your own relationship? Share your observations of traits you admire with your partner. Continue to observe qualities in other couples that you'd like to further develop in your own relationship, and continue to share your observations with your partner.

As we incorporate tools to deepen our relationship, including learning from our partner and from positive role models, we can experience more satisfaction and intimacy. And, as we give to each other from a fuller, more openhearted place, we'll have more love to contribute to our families and to the larger world.

conclusion:

HOW CAN I LOVE MORE?

When two people relate to each other authentically and humanly, God is the electricity that surges between them.

—*Martin Buber*

In relationship, 1+1=3. We see a good relationship this way: the space between a couple is its own entity. We like to refer to this expanded energy as a baby—the more love and care you give it, the more it grows, thrives, and evolves.

We identify four kinds of relationships, according to how well they are cared for and the levels of connectedness.

In the **first** kind of relationship there is a bare minimum of loving. One or both partners may have a foot out the door. They may be staying together only for practical reasons, such as money or children or fear of being alone. There may be considerable indifference, hostility, blame, loneliness, and little satisfaction. Walls have built up. There is not a lot of safety and trust or a sense that you are important to your partner. For this relationship to begin to evolve, the partners would need to learn tools to lower their reactivity such as those presented in the fifth heart tool, Commitment to Lower Reactivity. They'd need to make agreements to be kinder to each other, show more appreciation, and begin to take an interest in each other.

In the **second** kind of relationship, the couple pays enough attention to the partnership to take care of practical household matters and parenting, but they live like roommates, with separate lives emotionally. In this kind of relationship, each partner focuses on self: "What am *I* getting from the relationship?" There may be tension that comes out in excessive sarcasm and complaining but it doesn't get expressed constructively to bring about positive change. In this kind of relationship, partners keep the status quo and may not want to rock the boat.

When things go well, they get along, especially in public. But under stress, the partners revert to old, reactive coping patterns. There can be underground contempt and resentment, and partners may turn to people outside the relationship as sounding boards. Because conflict is often swept under the rug, fights can flare up suddenly. But because the couple doesn't have the tools to help them understand themselves and each other, they are unable to resolve their conflicts. For this couple to evolve, they would need to lower reactivity, become aware of their own and each other's feelings and needs. Many of the heart tools we've presented here can help this couple cultivate more connectedness and trust with each other. To name a few: PAL (Presence, Appreciation, and Listening), and Making Room for Differences.

In the **third** kind of relationship, you consider yourself good friends, are generally compatible, enjoy your family, and experience overall satisfaction. You are able to talk through and resolve most disagreements, work as a team when you need to, and enjoy some intimacy. But because the focus is not on personal and relationship growth, these relationships can become stagnant. You may begin to take each other for granted and then feel "something is missing." For this couple to evolve their level of intimacy, they need to make their relationship a priority, integrate the heart tools into their daily lives, have more fun together, and listen deeply to each other's emotional needs.

In the **fourth** kind of relationship, partners focus on growing as individuals and as a couple, in addition to enjoying friendship and passion. There is genuine partnership. You consciously see your partner as your teacher, helping you to learn through conflict, grow as a couple, and flourish as an individual. This is a rich and exciting form of intimacy. Your relationship is a priority. There is both a deep feeling of security and a feeling of unconditional love. You feel safe to be vulnerable. You have your partner's back and he/she has yours, and you strive to be loving toward your partner regardless of the challenges you face, both as individuals and as partners. You have made a mutual commitment to keep growing your capacity to love. This relationship also needs to be cared for on a regular basis. You deeply care about your partner's emotional well-being, and ask about it. Partners need to stay attuned to themselves and each other, through communication and time together.

It is also important to understand that the four kinds of relationships we've identified here are fluid. A bad argument can bring us to our knees, and make us feel like we are in the first level of relationship. Harsh words can easily break our partner's heart, and cause deep pain. We are all going to slip. But the more we develop our capacities to love ourselves and each other, we can use these capacities to take responsibility for the harm we cause, offer amends, and move forward.

Any step you take to be more loving is a big step: deciding not to be critical; no longer threatening to leave; not raising your voice; voicing your needs directly, instead of complaining and blaming; giving up the need to be right; expressing your truth even though you anticipate this might upset your partner; risking vulnerability by sharing fears and insecurities. No matter where you are, appreciate that you can step on to a path of change and growth whenever you decide to.

Making any changes to improve your relationship is an act of love and compassion. Wherever you are in your relationship, it is possible to evolve to another, more rewarding level. This chapter offers you inspiration and guidance to grow your relationship. The most effective way to do this is by turning inward and asking yourself: "What can *I* do to love more?"

Loving is about stretching beyond ourselves to give to another human being. It's not only about giving what you want to give but about giving what makes another person feel loved. This requires awareness and making the effort to move into a place where you want to give for the purpose of loving your partner. It is indeed living bigger than your own personality, ego, and fears.

Opening your heart is like climbing a mountain. It requires focus, commitment, determination, endurance, and persistence. There are no shortcuts to loving. Because it is so easy to fall in love, it seems it would be an equally simple matter to stay in love. But we all know that if you don't give attention and nutrients to a living thing, it will eventually die. Relationships are living entities—both your relationship with your partner and your relationship with yourself. They must be nourished to survive and grow.

Practices to Open Your Heart and Keep Your Partnership Vital

Notice your partner's beauty. Imagine picking up an oyster shell off the beach, opening it up, and finding a shining, translucent pearl inside. When we first met our partner we naturally were able to see the beauty within. We looked beyond the flaws and faults and saw their beauty.

The next time you're with your partner, take the time to notice his or her beauty. We do this when we look at a sunset and appreciate its magnificence. We do it when we look at the ocean and take in its roaring beauty. We do it when we look at the stars and see their diamond-like sparkle. We do it when we close our eyes and feel the wind caress our skin. These are ways we can touch the beauty of life. Try to see and sense your partner this way. It will transform your relationship. You will see your partner and your relationship as a precious jewel.

Gratitude. At the end of each day, make a list of all the things you are grateful for that day. We suggest making a list of at least five things you feel grateful for, such as your loved ones, your health, your home, your job, your sense of humor, life itself.

Left to its own devices, the mind tends to look for negative things to attach to. Gratitude is a wonderful way to reverse this process by tuning into and appreciating what you have. What is important is to be conscious of our gratitude. A wonderful practice is to fall asleep reflecting on the things we're grateful for. It can change the whole chemistry of our minds and bodies, as well as activating the energy in our hearts. When you practice gratitude, you're not denying the difficulties you may be experiencing. But reflecting on what you are grateful for allows you to take stock of these difficulties in a more objective way. We can get so bogged down in negative thoughts—regrets, anxieties, anger—that we are no longer present. Gratitude breaks through our anxiety and depression and brings us back into the moment.

Live with zest. Spend at least 10 to 15 minutes a day doing something that you are passionate about. This could be playing an instrument, singing, writing poetry, reading a book, taking a walk in the woods, biking, running, practicing yoga, meditation, talking to a friend, and listening or moving to music. When you are feeding your passions as an individual, you have more zest for life, and that zest will infuse your relationship. Do whatever creates excitement and passion for you. For us, right now, writing this book is opening our hearts because we are passionate about helping people create healthy, loving relationships.

Write it down. Try journaling for a few minutes each day. Journaling is a way to become more aware of our thoughts and feelings, and at the same time letting them go by putting them on paper. Many books about the journaling process are available. A favorite of Ani's is *The Artist's Way* by Julia Cameron. Journaling can support us in many different ways. Some people use it to clarify thoughts and feelings, while others journal to come up with new ideas. Still others use it as a daily practice to dive deeper into their consciousness. It's a tool that can open your heart.

Drop into stillness. A formal practice of meditation for 15 to 20 minutes a day can also open your heart. Meditation teaches us to witness our thoughts, feelings, and sensations and to become less attached to and identified with these parts of ourselves. As we drop into stillness and silence, we become aware of the moment. In this silent, nurturing space, we can hear our inner voice, touch our true nature, and be more connected to ourselves and all of life. In silence we don't have to focus on doing; we can focus on being.

Generosity. Another way to open your heart is to give to another living being. Giving is a direct act of love. The recipient can be a person, but it doesn't have to be. It could also be your pet, your houseplants, the perennials in your garden, or the birds in your back yard. The important thing is to open up and extend your nurturing heart energy to a living being. Opening your heart and giving is like putting a plug into a wall socket and turning on a switch—instantaneously, the energy flows. When we give to another being, we get back the energy of love many times in return. It doesn't matter who or what we love. It matters *that* we love.

Some people spend their whole lives waiting for the "perfect soulmate" to love. In the meantime, they miss out on giving love to themselves and to those who are already in their lives. The world is cheated when we don't give to others. Don't wait. By putting out loving energy, we are creating a more loving world to live in. The world needs each of our loving hearts.

No matter how you are feeling, no matter what is going on in your life, no matter how much physical or emotional pain you are experiencing, you can give to another being. Nancy, a successful, thirty-six-year-old businesswoman, came from a family riddled with drug addiction and alcoholism. She had never had a long-term intimate relationship and had pretty much decided to give up looking for a partner. Instead, she adopted a black, Labrador puppy. She got up early to take her pup on long walks in the park, and talked to her puppy and enjoyed him tremendously. It was by loving this puppy unconditionally that she started to open her heart to the possibilities of being in an intimate relationship with a man. A year later she met a man on a business trip, and two years later they married. She attributed her openness to a relationship to her experience with her beloved dog. She and her husband went on to have two children together.

Never underestimate the power that the act of

giving has to open the energy field inside of you. The problem never lies in the obstacles in life. The problem is *believing* that the obstacles stop us from loving and living. Basketball coach John Wooden, who won more consecutive games on the college level than any other coach, says the most important thing in life is love. He never talked to his players about winning games. He always talked about not getting caught in the ups and downs of the game. His bottom-line message: Do the best that you can, stay in the game of life, and love.

How many times have we not been in the mood to be kind, and yet we're in a situation where someone is kind to us, and that opens our heart?

Stretch to stay connected. Make the intention to stay connected even when your partner is angry, upset, or disappointed with you. When we feel blamed, it is very easy to become defensive and close our heart. This is when we need to return to our intention to grow our ability to love.

The most powerful and loving way to respond to someone who is upset is to listen to the hurt part of them, while staying connected to yourself. Allow yourself to simply be with them and try to understand their feelings from their perspective. We don't have to agree with them. We simply need to show up with as much presence and compassion as we can muster.

Tara and Jason had been trying to get pregnant with a second child. After a full year of trying, they finally succeeded. Then, three months into the pregnancy, Tara had a miscarriage. She was heartbroken and despondent, fearing that she'd never have the second child she longed for. Although Jason had agreed to have a second child, he was secretly relieved by the miscarriage. His business had sustained recent losses, and he was deeply anxious about being able to afford a second child.

Tara was devastated and, understandably, needed tremendous comfort. But Jason couldn't support her wholeheartedly. Because he wasn't feeling the same level of grief, he began to withdraw from his wife. She, in turn, was angry and hurt by his unemotional reaction. "How can you walk away from me at a time like *this*?" she cried. "You don't care about me!"

What ultimately helped Jason was understanding that he didn't have to have the same level of grief as his wife to be fully openhearted to her in *her* pain. In a pivotal session with them, we helped Jason put his practical and rational concerns aside for the moment, and simply attend to his wife's anguish. He spontaneously put his arm around her, and she sobbed in his arms. Both felt closer to each other.

When we keep our hearts open we can transform hurt into love. When we stretch to put ourselves in the other person's place we can feel a deep connection to the other person, as well as a connection to all suffering beings. We also feel more connected with ourselves. No matter how challenging the situation, we can remain open to love.

Loving in times of challenges such as illness and aging. Traditional marriage vows include the important reminder to love in times of sickness and health. This vow is not only about lovingly caring for the partner who is ill; it's also about the sick person treating his/her partner with as much kindness as possible. The challenge for most couples is not when things are going well but when one partner or both partners are having a difficult time. The challenge is to not bring your partner down to your level of discomfort and pain. This requires self-discipline and maturity. These challenges can offer times of intimacy deeper than we ever thought possible.

Joanne married Frank when she was forty and he was sixty. They fell head over heels in love. Their age difference was insignificant when they met. Frank was handsome, vigorous, and athletic. Both were runners and ran competitively. They also loved the outdoors, and their vacations took them to Europe on adventurous long bike trips. In his late seventies, Frank suffered a stroke, which limited his mobility. He could walk but no longer hike or bike. At this point, Joanne in her late fifties, was still running the Boston Marathon so they were now in very different places. It was an enormous adjustment for this couple to face the many ways Frank's stroke affected their relationship, especially their leisure time activities. Initially, they were stoic, and were afraid that talking about the changes would upset the other. But this created painful distance. Eventually, Joanne with the encouragement of a therapist, was able to talk with Frank about the loss of their active life together. It was a relief to both of them to finally talk openly about the pain they had each been holding alone. She was able to talk about her pain at no longer being able to share running with him and he was able to talk about his pain about his physical limitations. They made a recommitment to find new ways to enjoy time together. By talking about it, they moved from denial to acceptance of their present situation. The talks they had over several months, freed up energy for them to plan a new kind of vacation. Their most recent vacation was a cruise to the Mediterranean and North Africa. Joanne had ample time to workout in the gym on the boat and together they enjoyed the off-shore outings as well as the company of interesting people from around the world who shared the cruise with them.

One of the first questions that couples tend to ask us in their therapy sessions is, "Why do relationships have to be so hard?" The answer: To create anything of high quality, you need to put in a lot of work. Although relationships absolutely require effort, it actually takes even more energy to *avoid* working on your relationship. Avoidance is extremely stressful and draining.

Our intention for writing this book is to help you to have the best relationship you can have. We hope we have helped you on your way. We invite you to try out some of the practices we've presented here. When used regularly, we've seen them produce tremendous results. We recommend that you choose any of the heart tools and practices and use them each day for ninety days. We promise that you'll see a major change in your attitude and your behavior towards those you love. The more steps you take to live consciously and open your heart, the more you will experience the preciousness of life itself.

PUTTING HEART TOOLS INTO PRACTICE

Presence

Appreciation

Compassionate Listening

Making Room for Differences

Commitment to Lower Reactivity

**Transforming Hurt and Resentment
into Forgiveness**

Nurturing Passion

Seeing Your Partner as Your Teacher

How Can I Love More